New Perspectives   Personal and Professional Developme
                   Series Editor: Alan Maley

Teaching Myself

Bernard Dufeu

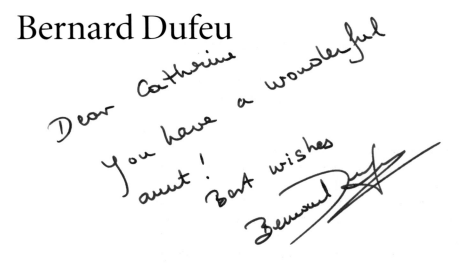

Dear Catherine
You have a wonderful
aunt! Best wishes
Bernard

Oxford University Press 1994

Oxford University Press
Walton Street, Oxford OX2 6DP

Oxford New York Toronto Madrid
Delhi Bombay Calcutta Madras Karachi
Kuala Lumpur Singapore Hong Kong Tokyo
Nairobi Dar es Salaam Cape Town
Melbourne Auckland

and associated companies in
Berlin Ibadan

Oxford and *Oxford English*
are trade marks of Oxford University Press.

ISBN 0 19 437 1883
© Oxford University Press 1994

Set in Adobe Minion and Minion Expert Set
by Wyvern Typesetting Limited

Printed in Hong Kong

To Marie
My companion in life, and on this enthralling journey.

Acknowledgements

We gratefully acknowledge the permission of James MacGibbon to reproduce the poem 'Tender Only to One' from *The Collected Poems of Stevie Smith* (Penguin 20th Century Classics) and of Warja Lavater for a photograph from *Le Petit Chaperon Rouge* (Adrien Maeght Editeur).

Although every effort has been made to secure all permissions prior to publication, if contacted, the publisher will be pleased to rectify any omissions at the earliest opportunity.

Contents

Author and series editor

BERNARD DUFEU has been teaching French at the University of Mainz in Germany since 1966. He is a teacher trainer and psychodramatist. His collaboration with Willy Urbain in an experimental course on 'Expression Spontanée' introduced him to new ways of teaching foreign languages and lead him to develop linguistic psychodramaturgy, described in this book.

He is the co-founder of the 'Centre de Psychodramaturgie' in Mainz, which trains teachers in linguistic psychodramaturgy.

ALAN MALEY worked for The British Council from 1962–1988, serving as English Language Officer in Yugoslavia, Ghana, Italy, France, and China, and as Regional Representative for The British Council in South India (Madras). From 1988–1993 he was Director-General of the Bell Educational Trust, Cambridge.

He wrote *Quartet* (with Françoise Grellet and Wim Welsing, OUP 1982). He has also written *Beyond Words, Sounds Interesting, Sounds Intriguing, Words, Variations on a Theme*, and *Drama Techniques in Language Learning* (all with Alan Duff), *The Mind's Eye* (with Françoise Grellet and Alan Duff), and *Learning to Listen* and *Poem into Poem* (with Sandra Moulding). He is also series editor for the Resource Books for Teachers and the Oxford Supplementary Skills.

Foreword

The title *Teaching Myself* is knowingly ambiguous, suggesting three interpretations which mesh neatly with central issues addressed in the book. *Teaching Myself* first of all suggests that the author himself is in a continual process of learning and development; that through his teaching he is teaching himself, and learning about that process. Secondly, *Teaching Myself* suggests that the author is, through the act of teaching, teaching what he is as a person; that he is not the disembodied bearer of a package of information and skills, but a fully-fledged personality, actively participating in the learning process along with his students. Finally, *Teaching Myself* has resonances for the students themselves, for they, as independent personalities, are ultimately responsible for their own learning—for 'teaching themselves'; the teaching–learning enterprise will be successful to the extent that teachers help their students to 'teach themselves'.

Linguistic Psychodramaturgy (LPD) draws its inspiration, on the one hand, from Moreno's Psychodrama, and, on the other, from action-oriented dramaturgy as practised by Augusto Boal, among others. LPD is a highly original blend but, lest its pedigree give rise to misleading impressions, it is worth emphasizing that it is pedagogically not therapeutically-oriented. This is not to say that it can be centrally applied by any teacher after simply reading this book. Any technique in the wrong hands can have undesirable effects. Teachers wishing to use LPD need special training, as the author frequently makes clear.

In fact, only a minority of teachers are likely to be in a position to apply LPD as an approach in its entirety. This by no means diminishes its claim on our attention, however, the case the author makes for a 'pedagogy of being', rooted in the here and now and responsive to the present and evolving needs of learners, is highly persuasive. It reminds us forcefully that learning is a physical and emotional experience, as well as an intellectual and rational one.

And the activities and procedures it describes are, in many cases, readily adaptable to non-LPD classrooms.

In reading *Teaching Myself* it is likely you find yourself 'teaching yourself' too.

ALAN MALEY

Introduction

This book brings together theory and practice. The two are closely intertwined: my hypotheses have affected how I work, just as my practical experience has given rise to new hypotheses. So the present work is the result of a productive interaction between thought and experience, both of which are still evolving and which, I trust, are far from reaching their full maturity. The book has been written to encourage thinking and criticism of the pedagogic process. Its open-ended character reflects the impossibility of recording a process that is in a permanent state of development.

Like images in a kaleidoscope, every reader will find different meanings and nuances, according to expectations, sensibility, and the state of personal development.

The book is written in the form of a triptych, so has three distinct 'panels' or parts:

The first part (Chapters 1 and 2) has to do with the 'why' of this approach, and describes the theoretical bases for linguistic psychodramaturgy, or LPD. Chapter 1 shows how language teaching moves progressively from a 'pedagogy of having' to a 'pedagogy of being', where the participant is at the centre of the learning process, and the main objective is to contribute to that person's development. Chapter 2 describes LPD's methodological concepts and considers areas of concern common to all language teachers: learning objectives, progression, comprehension, grammar, and retention.

The second part (Chapters 3 to 7) deals with the 'how' of this approach, showing how participants find their way to the heart of the foreign language, and experience it from within. In Chapter 3, we present two forms of relaxation (lying and sitting) in a way which allows teachers to use it at the beginning of their courses. In Chapter 4, we describe exercises for sensitizing participants to the rhythm and melody of the foreign language, connecting voice and movement to allow them to feel the peculiarities of the foreign language. Chapter 5 presents the main psychodramaturgy exercises (LPD), while Chapter 6 goes a step further into the world of the participants' imagination, using fairy-tales and myths. In Chapter 7, we give examples of creative reading and writing, which at the same time stimulate the students' imagination and expression.

The third part (Chapters 8 and 9) concentrates on the formation of trainers who want to respond to the disciplines of a pedagogy directed towards the personal development of the participants. This approach emphasizes training in human relations to help teachers perceive and understand their emotional responses in teaching situations. Chapter 8 returns in more detail to the reasons why teacher training takes place in three distinct phases, integrating personal and professional development and linking pedagogy and psychology; the same chapter also considers some aspects of this training from a new perspective, which is illustrated in Chapter 9.

This book may be read in any order, indeed its nine chapters can be read separately, according to the interests of each reader. Those with an interest in theory will, no doubt, turn to the first part, practising teachers to the second, and those with responsibility for teacher training to the third. The three parts are interwoven and complementary. So some readers may find it useful to begin by reading the development of LPD presented in Chapter 5 in order to understand more fully some of the methodological concepts described in Chapter 2.

While this book will allow some LPD techniques to be used in isolation, it cannot be a substitute for a training course. For that, direct training in linguistic psychodramaturgy is needed, especially in order to master the techniques used in the first few days, and to develop the attitudes that relate to them.

This book reflects a part of the author's personal and pedagogical development up to the time of writing. It records an important moment in a journey filled with hopes, doubts, and enthusiasms. This journey may have taken a new direction by the time the reader reads these lines, since like every living process, pedagogy is characterized by movement and change. By then, I may be treading new paths, or I may have embarked on new territories.

This book constitutes an 'invitation to travel'; for some, it will be a short journey, or a detour into the world that interests me, for others, a bridge that brings them to new pedagogical destinations.

Rather than provide a solid, nourishing diet I have set out to whet the appetite, to encourage teachers to experiment, to think in new ways, to look at their own behaviour, and in particular, to consider how far they allow other people to develop. Aspects of this book will, perhaps, enrich not only their use of new techniques, but also, and in particular, encourage new attitudes or new feelings.

In this work, I have tried to describe my views on learning and teaching. Although what I have written is essentially valid for me now, it cannot be a complete prescription for other people because every pedagogical choice is first and foremost a personal one. Henry Miller helps to show the road ahead:

> ... To be yourself, just yourself, is a great thing. And how does one do it, how does one bring it about? Ah, that's the most difficult trick of all. It's difficult just because it involves no effort.
> (Miller 1971)

I wish you good travelling, on your own road ...

PART ONE

The theoretical foundation of a pedagogy of being

1 Towards a pedagogy of being

1.1 From a pedagogy of having ...

The history of language teaching has seen many different approaches and methods (Howatt 1984). Whatever their apparent differences however, most of them share a similar view of the relationship between the learner and what is to be learnt. Essentially, the language is seen as knowledge to be transferred or transmitted to the learner.

This transfer is most often carried out through the use of a textbook. This has a dominant function, since it determines the situations, topics, structures, and vocabulary the learners will use. The main responsibility of the teacher is then to act as mediator between the learners and the textbook and to control the process.

The learners have no say in the process: they simply follow what has been pre-determined by others—textbook writers, publishers, etc. They therefore experience a twofold alienation: the language they

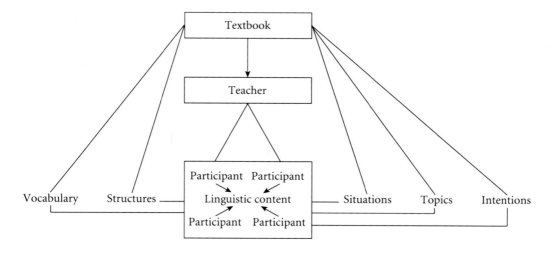

FIGURE 1   *The structure of teaching in a pedagogy of having*

are learning is not their own mother tongue, and what they say in it is not in their own words.

Characteristically, teaching takes place in two stages: learn first, then try to communicate. After understanding the text and carrying out the exercises, the learners are expected to use the language 'freely'. But, although in theory they have the right to express themselves at the end of the lesson, they can only use the words and structures which they have just learnt.

Memorization, based on the notion that 'the more you repeat, the more you retain', is a feature of most such approaches. Material is recycled in various ways ranging from the pattern drill to less obvious forms of repetition such as controlled role play.

Generally speaking, there is a set of learning objectives which are most often expressed in linguistic terms. The teaching/learning process is then directed towards finding the best way of achieving these objectives.

1.2 ... towards a pedagogy of being

Some would argue that the characteristics described above apply chiefly to *traditional* methods and that in the *communicative approach* they are less relevant.

While it is true that the communicative approach puts communication at the centre of the learning process[1] (i.e. learners are provided with the language as they need it), there are problems none the less:

— Excellent techniques are suggested, but in general there is a lack of a sense of unity in the activities: they do not link together to form a coherent learning progression. As a result, only a small minority of particularly creative teachers can use them in a sustained way.
— Creativity is often confused with absence of discipline, resulting in unprincipled eclecticism. In many cases, the activities are used simply as light relief or as a back-up to more traditional activities.
— Some teachers view the activity as good in itself without regard to its suitability for the group in question or the best time to use it.
— Some activities are based on mutually incompatible views of learning, which may foster contradictory attitudes.[2]
— Many activities are linear in nature and give insufficient opportunities for learners to express themselves in varied ways or to extend their repertoire. Teachers complain that 'they talk a lot but they don't seem to learn much'.

1 Some approaches have inaccurately been called communicative because they have retained a traditional methodology, and have simply added some communicative intentions and speech acts in order to help learners to master certain situations which are considered important. This is restricted to the linguistic aspect without any changes to how a language is learnt.

2 For instance, in *The Q Book* by Morgan and Rinvolucri, an exercise such as that on p.11 is a grammatical one with a veneer of personal involvement.

— The techniques are disconnected from a coherent and internally consistent methodology of language learning. This will be dealt with in Chapter 2.

Clearly, there is a need to introduce a note of rigour into this whole area without losing the creative energy which the communicative approach has undoubtedly sparked off. Equally, there is a need for training in the use of the approach—its methodology, techniques, and human relations implications. We will return to this in Chapters 8 and 9.

1.3 Characteristics of a pedagogy of being

To educate a child is not to fill a vase, it is to kindle a fire.
[MONTAIGNE]

Let us take one activity to illustrate the characteristics of this pedagogy. It is a technique drawn from Michel Fustier, called *L'année sabbatique (The year off)* in which each participant in the class describes what he or she would do with a year entirely free of work (Fustier 1978: 9). After trying out this exercise several times in order to find out how it might be developed, we have made it both broader and narrower: for example, participants are free to spend as much money as they like—but not to go on a world tour.

To introduce this activity, we invite the participants to close their eyes and spend five minutes imagining what they would do during their year off. Then, when they have reopened their eyes, we tell them that their year has ended. Readers interested in grammar will notice at this point that the participants will speak in the past tense throughout. The reason for this transposition into the past has no grammatical purpose; the imagination is more strongly stimulated when we talk about something that is supposed to have happened than when we talk about something that might happen in the future: for example, no one can answer 'I don't know' because the action has already taken place. Thanks to this device, the imagination is strongly reinforced.

We then ask a participant to choose two 'radio journalists' from the class to interview him or her about what happened during the past year. While the others listen to the 'broadcast' they can phone in to ask questions of their own. A third journalist makes a note of problems as they crop up (language errors, new vocabulary, words used by a participant which others may not know, etc.). These language problems are discussed after the interview, which gives everyone the chance to make notes without holding up the exercise. Then another participant is interviewed, and so on.

This exercise can lead equally well to a written exercise, for instance, to an article about the interview, or an account of one day's events as if described in a diary.

At this stage we use an outline activity, that is, an activity that provides a frame for words only: participants decide for themselves what goes inside. Contact with the language comes from the contact between each other in the chosen activity. *The individual participants and the group as a whole produce their own study plan from within themselves.* Whatever linguistic resources individuals may lack are provided by other participants or the teacher as 'animator'. So language develops in proportion to the students' needs and wishes of expression, and instead of eliciting responses we respond to a demand.

The language becomes relational, not functional. It enables the participants to express themselves and identify where they are in relation to themselves, to others, and their surroundings; it helps interpersonal communication between members of the group.

Dialogue begins as everyone reacts to the situation that arises out of the outline activity. The questions are true questions because the only person who knows the answer is the person to whom they are addressed; they have a real function in asking for precision, clarification, or information, so the means of communication takes on an authentic character.

As far as possible, the outline activity suggested by the 'animator' will be based on their assessment of the physical, affective, and intellectual life of the group. The activity will therefore reflect the dynamism, sensibility, and interests of the participants and offer the opportunity of a direct or symbolic transposition of the topics the participants introduce. The participants can involve themselves according to their perception of their real and their imaginary worlds (using personal experience and knowledge but also their potential at the time for projecting themselves).

A pedagogy of being concerns *the present* and *the presence* and tries to take account of the circumstances of participants in the group. It does not aim to provide a never-ending preparation for being, but direct and immediate action, and language is used as *a means of meeting in the here and now,* whether in the real world or in the world of the imagination.

Content is not imposed on participants from outside, it rises up from within them. It is not defined in the past by other people, but in the present by the participants themselves.

The activities include a double interest: the first which is intrinsic, so that we can enjoy the activities for what they are, even in our own language, outside the context of learning a foreign language; the other which is linguistic, because the activities allow participants to broaden their linguistic competence. Their interest in the activities is as people, not just as learners.

In this way, we can awaken or stimulate in the participants the needs, desires, and interests they have inside them. To be creative signifies above all to be in contact with one's desires, so that creativity can build a bridge to the other banks of the self.

Listening to one another is a very intense activity since no one can predict what will be said, and a topic is interesting in itself. Listening is directed towards the speaker but also towards the meaning of that person's message; it is not merely a case of listening to *someone's words* but to *someone*. The message is therefore understood in relation to the speaker. There is space for the unexpected, the surprising, and for originality, all of which encourages an awakening of curiosity.

Participants are affected by what they say and by what is said to them. There is a link between the interlocutors and their own speech because they are directly implicated. They can also feel themselves challenged by the speech of others. Each of us is the creator and therefore the author of his or her own speech.[3] Language is, among other things, a symbolic reflection and expression of the interior world of each participant, as well as of the group and the reactions between its members.

Language cannot be separated from its use; it has a personal resonance for each user. Participants can therefore take possession of a language and integrate it so well that it becomes their own. The language is then no longer entirely foreign even if they do not know the words, because when they experience it they are in direct contact with the words.

Rather than being identified as the objective of teaching, language thus becomes a medium of expression and communication. It contributes to the personal expression of the participants and the group, and facilitates contact between them. It is lived and experienced instead of being learnt in an abstract and alienating way. Contact with the language occurs through contact between the interlocutors. In other words, it is learnt through relation and interaction.

From the anonymity of the interlocutor who can be changed at will according to the didactic needs of the teacher, we move on to a

3 In order to encourage participants to express themselves it is not necessary, it seems to us, to resort to some Moskowitz-style exercises (Moskowitz 1978) which can transform the pedagogic setting into one of therapy, chiefly in order to satisfy the quest for sensation of some teachers who are carried away because they have been able to 'make something happen'.

style of communication where the participants express themselves because they have something to say to each other, and the dialogue is based on a real or imaginary situation, expression that is *direct* or *symbolic*.

Similarly, the connotative values of the language are taken into account, because they constitute an important part of the message. The tonality of what is said and the order in which things are said influences the meaning of the message. Comprehension is conveyed more forcibly through the *meaning of the message* than the sense of the words. The suprasegmental elements of the message (rhythm, melody, etc.) contribute to this comprehension (Chapter 2: 2.6 and Chapter 4).

The following example may help to illustrate the difference between sense and meaning.

The *sense* of a statement such as 'Are you coming this evening?' corresponds to a question asking whether or not the interlocutor is able or wants to come. Its *meaning* can be quite different, depending on the relations between the people concerned. If the phrase is spoken by someone in a higher position of authority, it may have the value of an order. If it is spoken by a close friend, it can be an invitation to spend a pleasant evening together. If there has been a disagreement, it may represent an offer of reconciliation. *Meaning* is defined by the context and the relationship between the speakers. The statement is an exchange, not just of words, but of a message.

Coming to understand what the message means is made easier by the fact that there is a close relationship between the speaker and his or her words, between the situation in the group and the expression of the participants, and by the fact that there is a close correspondence between what is said and what is expressed. Once signification has been reintroduced, the language is complete and comes fully to life.

The process of comprehension is itself modified and partly reversed. In traditional teaching it is largely the student's responsibility to learn what the teacher, or textbook, chooses. But, in a pedagogy of being it is mainly up to the 'animator' to grasp what the participants want to say. This is not just linguistic; the 'animator' must take a lead from the participants, instead of expecting them to follow the programme he or she, or the author of a textbook, has worked out.

The participants acquire the language by using it to express themselves and communicate. It is an *acquisition process* and not an act of learning. Just as we acquired, rather than learnt, our mother tongue, this process takes place, not in disorder, but in another order—one which meets the needs of expression of the participants.

The hierarchial, and therefore vertical transmission of *intellectual understanding* is replaced by a horizontal expansion of *practical knowledge* based on experience—horizontal because the participants contribute directly to its development. By this means, the *quality* of what is communicated is of another order, since it depends on another mode of apprehension.

We can illustrate this difference by comparing the intellectual understanding we have about a country after reading a book about it, and the practical knowledge we acquire from travelling in that country. This difference plays an important role in relation to language. It is also significant in relation to the retention of language since the type of initial contact one has with something unknown or new affects how one remembers it. Indeed, in certain cases we cannot know things unless we experience them. I cannot have an intellectual understanding of good wine. I can experience it as good; then I know it and I can remember it.

With this approach we begin to see the transition from a pedagogy of having, centred on an accumulation of intellectual understanding, to a pedagogy of being, directed towards knowledge from experience. The members of a class merely function as learners in a pedagogy of having, but they become *participants* in a pedagogy of being since it is with their person and their personality that they participate in the agreed activities.

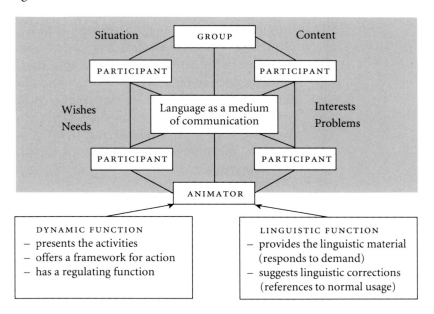

FIGURE 2   *The structure of learning in a pedagogy of being*

Responsibility for the course content and its development are shared because the participants have joint responsibility: the teacher no longer bears the weight of a fixed programme that has to be carried out. The teacher's role is transformed from principal and leading actor to producer, no longer teaching but animating. This is why we talk of 'animators' rather than 'teachers', in the etymological sense of the word (*Anima* = breath, life) because animators breathe life into language and contribute to the dynamism of the group's life. The animator has a dual role, dynamic on the one hand, linguistic on the other.

The atmosphere on the course allows creativity to germinate and blossom. Participants can feel more at ease in the group because there is a climate of personal and linguistic acceptance.

In fact, in the world of the imagination there is no right, wrong, or better response—just personal response. It is as if, for instance, each participant preferred a different colour according to their own taste and without reference to any external influence: blue would not be considered better than red.

The group comes to accept the absence of positive or negative value judgements in response to what is expressed 'It isn't good, or bad, or better—it just *is*!' Each participant has a personal response to the situation presented, which leads to a general atmosphere of 'That's OK'.

So far as linguistic accuracy is concerned, errors are viewed as indispensable to learning, since there can be no learning without error. Fear of being embarrassed by one's mistakes can be reduced or overcome in this atmosphere. A predisposition to learn can be transformed into a willingness to experience and explore the possibilities and limitations of the foreign language. Participants are encouraged to take risks within a reassuring framework; this inspires in them a feeling of safety and confidence.

The following table summarizes the main differences between the two approaches:

a pedagogy of having	a pedagogy of being
WHO	WHO
Learner	Participant
Teacher	Animator

HOW	HOW
Hierarchical relationship	Empathetic relationship
Teacher imposes, controls, demands responses	Animator suggests, accompanies, responds to demand
Vertical transmission of intellectual understanding	Horizontal expansion of practical knowledge
Teaching on a conscious level	Conscious and unconscious learning
Voluntary act of learning	Acquisition process
Act of memorizing, repetition	Process of discovery, exploration, experimenting
Language learnt, transmitted by textbooks	Language lived, approached through experience
Teacher responsible for course programme and content	Animator and participants share responsibility for development of the programme and content
Learner responsible for his/her mistakes	Mistakes indispensable to acquisition
Situation imposed from outside and constructed according to didactic criteria	Real or imaginary situation emerges from within the group
Programmed	Individualized
Speaker, separated from his/her speech content, results in double alienation	Speaker expresses himself/herself in direct contact with his/her words
Pedagogy separated from (real) life	Life within the pedagogy

WHAT	WHAT
Language pre-selected, remote from group, programmed	Language spontaneous, emerges from within the group, individualized
Language of 'he', 'she', 'they' on meaning of the words	Language of 'I', 'we', 'you', centred on the significance of the message
Language has referential and metalinguistic function	Language has expressive, communicative, investigative, and symbolic function

PURPOSE	PURPOSE
Linguistic objectives	Personal and linguistic objectives
Functional	Development of the individual
Directed towards past or future	Directed towards the group
Pedagogy focused on an objective, on results	Pedagogy focused on a process

FIGURE 3   *From a pedagogy of having ... to a pedagogy of being*

1.4 The concept of the person in a pedagogy of being

A passer-by asks three bricklayers what they are doing.
The first says 'I'm putting bricks one on top of the other'.
The second declares 'I'm building a wall'.
The third replies 'I'm making a home for a family'. [ANON]

What we teach is not limited to content: we also teach communication and therefore human relations. It is important that we ask ourselves what sorts of relationships we are fostering, what image we have of people and of the self in the learning process.

1.4.1 The concept of the relationship between the self and pedagogy

Acquiring a language cannot be dissociated from the individual who is its subject. We cannot behave as though we were simply transferring content, and leave the participant's personality to one side on the pretext that he or she is 'in a learning situation'. What we do as teachers has an impact on the participants and therefore on their learning. The pedagogic act is always more than a simple act of teaching. Whatever approach we take to the foreign language, even the most traditional, we are always teaching more than just the language. What is at stake goes beyond linguistic learning: it relates to the self-confidence of the participants as well as their intellectual and personal development. We exert an influence by reinforcing, developing, or taking away from their attitudes and behaviour.

Every learning process is a process of change. It follows that we can develop or reinforce those forms of communication which lead to increased conformism and fixed ways of thinking. Alternatively, we can contribute to a process of personal discovery and development. It is, therefore, very important to consider what types of behaviour we create or encourage in the way we teach. It would be inappropriate, for example, to use alienating methodological procedures, based on a mechanistic concept of learning, to encourage the participants' autonomous personal development.

Our pedagogic approach, therefore, does not separate learning from living. The process of learning plays an integral part in the overall development process of the individual. Life does not stop as we enter the classroom door; there is no artificial frontier between life on the outside and life inside the classroom. Learning is a living act which encompasses the life of those who take part in it. So we cannot maintain a sort of professional myopia, and consider only the linguistic aspects of what we teach. The participant's individuality is at the centre of this pedagogy. The participant engages in the learning process as an individual, and the act of learning contributes to his or her personal development.

The participant is a unique being and his or her speech will reflect this. Activities must allow each participant to contribute a personal response by giving expression to his or her uniqueness. The activities should respect and encourage the development of the participant's individuality and so contribute to the individual process of personal evolution. This pedagogy, then, is founded on a dynamic concept of the individual in evolution.

All individuals are known and accepted with their polarities, including doubts and certainties, weaknesses and strengths, self-denial and expectations, fears and desires, terrors and dreams, a wish for both stability and movement, a need to be both dependent and autonomous. The conjunction of all these forces reveals the richness of the individual and the dynamism of his or her action. It is by integrating these forces that each person accepts all aspects of his or her own personality.

Some learning processes have the effect of removing an individual's 'shadows', those personal traits which are precisely what can give relief. At the same time, they claim the right to question the person as a whole. But this image of mankind is sterilized and stunted. They create an atmosphere of artificial happiness in which the student is treated like a child. It is not surprising that so much emphasis is placed on surface appearances, and such learning processes are often characterized by frenzied activities in an attempt to enliven the class.

The process of acquisition through experience is a process of personal development. A dancer does not just learn the steps and movements of a dance: the main task is at a deeper level, to develop suppleness, flexibility of harmony, and equilibrium. It is the same in pedagogy: what we do is not purely linguistic in character, it relates to behaviour. We have to develop the attitudes, aptitudes, and forms of behaviour needed to learn a language, above all receptiveness and a capacity for expression (Chapter 2: 2.6). We each have these aptitudes but sometimes they have been locked away or buried as a result of our education or social surroundings. Sometimes they have remained inside us waiting for the chance to grow. As we shall see in the second part of this book, many activities can be used to develop these key aptitudes, and while this is happening the participants are simultaneously acquiring the language.

A pedagogy of being is concerned far less with the question 'How do I teach a defined content?' than with two other questions:

— 'How do I create the necessary conditions for acquiring a language?'
— 'How can I facilitate the development of each participant's receptiveness and capacity of expression in order that they can acquire the foreign language?'

Our approach is trying to create a pedagogy free from narrow functional objectives, in which each participant follows a personal path using a personal rhythm, and is accepted at whatever stage he or she happens to be in personal and linguistic development. There are no external norms. In this way, we avoid attempts to stereotype the individuals or the group. We move from a ready-made to a made-to-measure pedagogy, in which content changes to suit the person, and not the other way round. There is a shifting of pedagogic values. The process of acquisition becomes more important than the product, the path more important than the destination.

Our aim as 'animators' is to learn alongside the participants, taking care not to impose our own demands concerning some remote or uncertain future, since it is not a matter of pushing participants to reach the end without having first experienced the process. Each participant is the subject of his or her own learning and not the object of our projects, desires, or intentions. Instead of teaching, we educate; instead of imposing, we propose; instead of pointing the way, we accompany. Like mountain guides, we put our knowledge and experience at the service of our clients during the journey they are making. For language acquisition, this approach means that each participant will make progress at a personal rate in relation to what has already been learnt and the echo from the language expressed in the sessions. Each is therefore free to continue along a private and unique path.

This new perspective explains, among other things, the conceptual changes which occur as a response to difficulties found in learning. In a pedagogy of having, the learner starts from an assumed or actual standard, and the activities are built around objectives to be achieved; each error is viewed as an obstacle in relation to those objectives. In our pedagogy, error is an integral part of the acquisition process. Wanting to avoid error can interrupt acquisition, and can even prevent it. This is why we try to create an atmosphere which not only allows people to experiment without fear of error, but in which error is valued, since it is the means by which people become aware of the possibilities and limitations of the language.

1.4.2   An approach to the whole person

In the acquisition process each participant is involved physically, affectively, and intellectually within a social and spiritual context.

Physical involvement

The body is directly involved in a number of exercises: relaxation (Chapter 3), breathing, vocalization, rhythm, and poetry with movement (Chapter 4). In some warm-ups we use a progression which goes from gesture to the voice (sounds and interjections) to the verbal, as we do in group exercises where the language is strongly supported by gesture, for example, in the group mirror exercise (Chapter 5: 5.2.1).

In addition, exercises such as the variation on *the mirror* (Chapter 5: 5.2.2) or *Dialogue without words* (Chapter 5: 5.3.1), begin with purely physical expression followed by vocal and verbal expression.

Affective involvement

Talking is, of course, an act of involvement. In linguistic psychodramaturgy, or LPD, this involvement is concerned with both *content* and *relationships*.

Content is determined by the participants themselves so that they are directly or symbolically associated with what they and others say. It becomes *their* speech. Directly or symbolically, their inner life finds its own expression in the foreign language. Interestingly, speaking in another language often affords an individual greater freedom of expression than is readily accepted in their own language.

Participants tend to feel particularly vulnerable when learning a foreign language and this can affect *relationships*. They may be afraid of appearing foolish in front of others and feel frustrated if they are not able to express their feelings or thoughts with sufficient nuances. Speaking with a limited vocabulary makes some people feel slow and therefore 'stupid'. It is important to remember that some participants will not speak at all because they are so afraid of failing to speak correctly.

Doubling techniques (Chapter 5: 5.2.1), and other techniques which involve sequences, can be used to support participants in their expression, to enlarge their skills where they feel the need and to progressively build self-confidence.

The small size of groups—never more than twelve members— makes it possible for members to identify strongly with each other, and favours the cohesion of the group while still leaving room for diversity. The atmosphere created by the exercises and the type of relationships encouraged by the style of the animator's guidance, help to build self-confidence further by providing a more relaxed attitude towards errors or 'blind-spots'.

Involvement of the intellect

The intellect is not simply busy with cognitive and conscious activities, the sort which arise with language problems, such as from written exercises or explanations requested by a learner after correction of a language point. Unconscious intellectual activities, subconscious generalization processes, synthesis, organization of knowledge, comprehension by intuition or deduction, are all taking place while acquisition is happening. Conceptual intelligence and intuition are stimulated by an attitude of discovery and experimentation in the foreign language which we try to develop in courses, and in activities which appeal to the participants' imaginations.

When participants 'live' the language directly, for example, as protagonists during an activity, we often notice aspects of conscious work on the language, as in the way they react to a suggested correction; acquisition seems to take place as a more direct process. On the other hand, for participants acting as 'assistants', for example as listeners, conscious cognitive activities through a sensitive observation of the functioning of the language can take place in a more detached way because they are not directly involved in the action taking place. This may explain why linguistic corrections suggested by animators, even when they are not taken up by protagonists who are too caught up in the heat of action, do have an important function; they can have a resonance for other members of the group.

In this way, intellectual understanding is not ignored but neither is it accorded the exclusive place it can often occupy in traditional teaching.

For ease of presentation we have separated the body, the emotional self, and the intellect, but clearly they influence each other and are interdependent. For example, suppressing the emotions has an impact on intellectual development, reduces receptive, open attitudes, and sets up a defensive barrier that inhibits the working of the mind. For its part, the intellect can channel emotional overflows. There is no doubt that a complementary and free association of these three functions is the best environment for language acquisition.

The social dimension

Participants begin by discovering their emotional selves, tuning in to their sensations, feelings, needs, desires, and interests, their temporary or long-term limitations. In this way, they prepare for listening more sensitively, for accepting and respecting others—like the mother who said at the end of a two-week intensive course, that she understood her children in a different way when they came home from school, or another who said her children had a different quality of listening, that she felt a different atmosphere when she read them a bedtime story. So, during the great adventure of discovering foreign language, participants also work together on relationships and the kinds of communication they have with each other. Sometimes this gives them a different and broader view of life, or a more accurate and at times transformed perception of themselves, other people, and their environment (as in the case of one unemployed man who regained his self-confidence through the course).

The spiritual dimension

The symbolic significance of the LPD exercises, and the real and imaginary worlds they bring to life, can activate new conceptions of relationships, communications, mankind, and life for both participants and animators.

1.4.3   Imagination as a primary source of expression of the self

Reality is just one example of the possible, and therefore can be imagined differently. [DÜRRENMATT]

We have noted that classical and pragmatic forms of teaching may give little room to the here and now. More traditional forms of education look towards the past while some newer ones look to the future. There is no need for this gap between time, place, and language. It is possible to be in direct touch with the present, to concentrate on the *now*, to express the present directly or symbolically in a verbal sequence, or let the participant say spontaneously whatever comes to mind, and to make it the object of a monologue or a dialogue. We do this at the beginning of an LPD course. It prepares each participant for being in contact with the self and for expressing at will what is felt or comes spontaneously to mind. We shall examine this type of expression in more detail in Chapter 5.

We also make use of our imagination. It is always there, latent, and ready to come to the surface. It can, at any moment, enlarge the reality about us. We only have to discover the way to reach it and respect some of the laws which govern it. Using our imagination we can reach the symbolic, the mysterious, the strange, and the poetic that is inside us all. In this way, we can stimulate the pleasures of existence, of dreaming and wishing, which enthuse our desire for expression.

Since imagination occupies such a central place in LPD, it is important to understand some of the principles on which our approach is based, and to describe some of the effects of those exercises which involve imagination. With the help of each participant and the group as a whole, it is possible to create another reality, a different scene, which comes alive in their imaginations. By introducing imagination into language acquisition we create a protected space or, to borrow Winnicott's phrase, 'an intermediate space' (Winnicott 1971). This gives participants a freedom of expression which allows them to be someone else and thus explore all the imaginative potential that lies untapped within them.

The classroom becomes a creative space in which two scenes are superimposed: one is the solid reality of the classroom itself, the other, resulting from the activity, enables you be someone else while still being yourself, under the cover of the imaginary world: 'It isn't me, it's just a product of my imagination' (Mannoni 1969). The imaginary setting—an island, for instance, a castle or a cloud—can bring about a symbolic expression of the real or imaginary life of the group. A relational reality emerges in the contact between people (the participants) and characters (the roles they play).

The imagination opens out the field of expression and at the same time gives it a symbolic depth which is reflected in the expression of the participants.

We achieve a 'multi-dimensionality' of expression. In this creative space, using their imaginations, participants come much closer to

themselves and each other than by repeating the often dull exercises
in some language teaching textbooks.

   This invitation to travel in the world of the imagination constitutes
an invitation not only to *be*, but to *be more*.

   The real and the imaginary worlds meet across a second dimension
in *the place of creation and experiment* which constitutes what
Winnicott called a 'potential space'.

   There is a real space, the classroom, on to which the imaginary
space of the scene to be enacted (e.g. the earthly paradise) will be
superimposed. Each influences the other.

   In real time, 10 a.m. is replaced by theatrical time, e.g. an evening
in Spring.

   Real people meet each other through imaginary people: Paul, playing the part of the Serpent, meets Maria, playing the part of Eve.

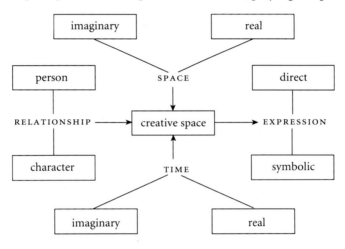

FIGURE 4   *Enlarging reality through imagination and symbolism*

1.4.4   Creativity as a means of contributing to personal development

To help understand why we integrate imagination into our pedagogy
of being, we are going to explain why creativity is important in pedagogy, especially in relation to the acquisition of languages. If we consider the pedagogic act as an act of development of the individual, it
is important to see what part creativity plays in this development.
Contact with the participants' imaginations directly influences the
development and strength of their identity.

   To be creative is to make a personal response in a particular situation. It is an original response because it originates in us. Our perception of ourselves is strengthened because we live differently in the creative act and experience details we cannot perceive in everyday life. Sometimes in this creative act we individualize ourselves most of all, and can be most fully ourselves, unrestrained by external contingencies. An experimental field opens up inside us, and drawing from our unconscious we can symbolically express a part of our psychic reality. This is one reason why a well-chosen activity using imagination activates participants and stimulates their desire to express thoughts and ideas.

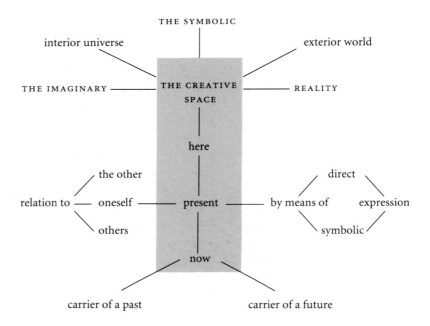

FIGURE 5   *The multi-dimensionality of the field of expression in a pedagogy of being*

In the creative space, the inner universe and the exterior world, the conscious and the unconscious, meet and are expressed.

The participants and the group project their wishes and needs of expression through an outline activity.

The here and now are experienced through a multi-dimensional present that is increasing in size and energy. They not only represent a material reality but are invested with problems, preoccupations, memories, disappointments, satisfactions, desires, needs, interests, expectations, hopes ...

To enter the imagination is to contact parts of oneself, worlds within oneself, which have a character of otherness. This can help in building a bridge to other participants, and in recognizing both their interior richness and the variety of worlds they carry inside them, worlds which cannot always find their expression in day-to-day existence. The result may be a broader and more flexible acceptance of others. Thanks to activities which stimulate the imagination, inter-group relations are often profound and intense. Potential relational bridges between participants can find their expression in the imagination, yet leave each person free to decide upon the distances they wish to maintain.

Developing the participants' perception and acceptance of others, of their originality and inevitable differences, also encourages an attitude of openness towards what is strange, and towards unfamiliar cultures; this process helps in learning a foreign language.

We create our world according to our perception of reality. However, as Korzybski (1941) observes, 'The map is not the territory', i.e. our representation of reality is not the same as reality itself.

Creation begins with looking at things differently. Through creative activities we learn to establish new relationships between things, and to perceive different aspects of reality; this can lead to a broadening or restructuring of our perception of reality.

This change in perception, this fresh perspective, often provides a basis for change and helps bring about a different attitude to our reality. Instead of accepting things as they are, we start to act upon them and to develop innovative attitudes. We can take part in the creation of our own future instead of accepting it in advance as given, predestined or determined by others, and by circumstances. The imagination therefore constitutes a catalyzing and metabolizing force. Confidence in the face of the new and unknown grows; a certain curiosity for the unknown and the unusual develops. A bridge is built between the interior and external worlds, which helps towards a better control over reality, and an enrichment both of experience and the capacity for living.

1.4.5 Creativity as a means of contributing to the acquisition of language

To talk is a creative, rather than a repetitive or simply imitative, act. Learning a foreign language is also a creative process. When we use techniques to stimulate creativity or activate the imagination, we simultaneously develop mental aptitudes and processes needed in language learning.

4 We are indebted to Willy Urbain for the use of 'neutral' masks, which we employ only in the first phases of the course of study, the transference of the psychodrama techniques of *the double* and *the mirror* into the pedagogy of languages, the principles of the intervention of a third person, which we find in *the triadic relationship* (though in a different form from the one he had advocated) as well as the principle of *the postponed meeting* and *the direct meeting* (though we have radically transformed its original setting). I also owe to him a number of theoretical foundations relating to these exercises (Urbain 1972).

We can, for instance, sharpen our senses of observation and curiosity, widen our capacity for abstraction, train ourselves to create new relationships or new co-relations between given elements; we can learn to relax our habitual patterns of thought and be more flexible. We can develop our readiness to learn and experiment. We can learn to widen, extend, or vary our strategies for action. We can train ourselves to face up to new situations and so to restructure or transfer reality. At the same time, an open attitude to the new, the unknown, and sensitivity towards other modes of perception will be stimulated. In addition, playing in and with the language brings about a different relationship with it.

Training in creativity and the activation of the imagination contributes to the enlarging of participants' capacity for expression, and therefore of their communicative competence in the foreign language. A pedagogy of being not only encompasses the participant during his or her development, but has a direct effect on that development.

1.5 An application of the pedagogy of being: psychodramaturgy

Every learning process is an experiment.

We are now going to introduce the application stage of the pedagogy of being, which constitutes the central object of this book: linguistic psychodramaturgy (LPD). We provide its sources here, and in Chapter 2 we describe its methodological foundations, and devote the second part of this book to a presentation of its practical implementation.

1.5.1 Sources of psychodramaturgy

The term *psychodramaturgy* refers to *psychodrama* and *dramaturgy*, its two principal sources.[4] We shall try to describe LPD by reference to where it corresponds or differs from them.

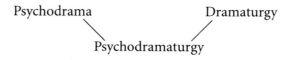

The sources have been adapted to the pedagogic context of language learning. We do not provide therapy or theatre, but we use foundations and techniques which stem from these two areas, just as actors or sports people refer to other disciplines, such as relaxation and visualization, to improve the quality of their performance.

Psychodrama: an approach through action

Let us consider first of all what we owe to psychodrama. It was created in the 1920s by Moreno, who also developed role playing and, subsequently, sociometrics. In psychodrama, the patient is referred to as the protagonist, or 'principal actor' in the tradition of Greek theatre. Instead of talking about problems, the protagonist converts them into action during group sessions. For this, the protagonist chooses from the group those participants who can take on the roles of the other actors in his or her drama. These are 'antagonists': parents, partners, colleagues, etc. The protagonist 'produces' the situation he or she wants in order to clarify or transform. This is therefore an experimental rediscovery of the experienced by experiencing. This enactment permits the situation to be re-lived and viewed afresh in order to develop an awareness of deep sources of conflicts or tensions and to start to control the situation using psychodramatic techniques.

In *linguistic psychodramaturgy* (LPD) something similar occurs. Little or nothing is said about the language, at least to begin with, which is not taught in abstraction but experienced *at first hand,* and develops through communication.

The concept of creative spontaneity

This is one of the fundamental concepts of psychodrama:

> Learning to be spontaneous is an important discipline and should be demanded of all teachers and therapists in our institutions. Their duty is to awaken and strengthen the spontaneity of their students and patients. (Moreno 1987: 46)

According to Moreno, creativity is latent in each of us and can be activated by the catalyzing action of spontaneity.

The concept of creative spontaneity is also fundamental to LPD. For the expression of the participants to be spontaneous, the content should not be fixed in advance but born out of the participants and the group. For us, therefore, spontaneity excludes all precise programming of content, which is why every LPD activity begins with an outline activity, an open framework which participants fill in according to their wishes of expression. Texts are used mainly as 'triggers' or as warm-up activities for a topic (Chapter 7: 7.1.1, 7.1.2, 7.1.4). The development of creative spontaneity lets participants express themselves personally and directly in the foreign language.

For spontaneity to play a successful role as a catalyst of creativity it is necessary to make use of what Moreno calls 'warm-ups' (Moreno 1970: 17–25). This concept is used throughout LPD: every key exercise is preceded by a warm-up exercise which prepares the protagonists for taking part in what follows. This might be a game with the rhythms and melody of the language, or it may involve listening to the other person. It might also prepare participants to carry out the exercise itself; the warm-up for *the triadic relationship* (Chapter 5: 5.2.3), for example, requires that participants concentrate on themselves and let gestures and language come to them spontaneously—which is what they will be asked to do in the exercise itself. Because of this advance preparation, the group feels able to carry out the exercise on their own.

We also 'warm-up' aptitudes, attitudes, types of behaviour, and acquisition mechanisms. It can be assumed that one part of the significant effects of LPD on acquisition is due to the fact that, through these techniques, we draw on resources originally developed when we were acquiring our first language. Techniques of language acquisition which may lie dormant within us are reactivated to facilitate the acquisition of the foreign language.

The concept of encounter

The notion of 'encounter' has been one of Moreno's main themes: one of his first books was called *Einladung zu einer Begegnung (Invitation to an encounter, 1915).*

LPD constitutes an invitation to an encounter through the foreign language. Different levels of encounter reflect the relational progression in LPD: there are encounters with oneself, then with another or others, and the environment (Chapter 2: 2.3.3). This is where the foreign language fulfils its function as a medium of relations, communications, and interactions, and therefore of encounter between the participants. Encounter is helped by the small size of the group and by the congruence between the language of the participants and their own individuality.

> People bring all their strengths and weaknesses to the encounter, charged with spontaneity and creativity; the encounter lives in the here and now. (Moreno 1987: 129)

The notion of 'here and now' is to be taken in its broadest sense (Figure 5). This means that in addition to their present sensations, emotions, and needs, participants also bring their memories with their past, *and* the future dimension—their hopes and desires.

Consciously and unconsciously they express themselves in the language which springs up spontaneously.

The technical contribution of psychodrama

We have borrowed three fundamental techniques from psychodrama: *the double, the mirror,* and *role-reversal.* However, there are some basic differences in how we use them pedagogically.

The double

In psychodrama, one person acting as 'the double' stands behind the protagonist, adopting the same body attitude and verbalizing whatever the protagonist is unable to express. In LPD, we continue the technique of psychodrama, as described above, but there is a difference in form and function.

In psychodrama, the double tries to express what the protagonist either blocks, or holds back, or what he or she has difficulty in expressing. Occasionally, the double may even be confrontational in order to help the protagonist emerge from the blockage situation, or become aware of some aspect of a personal attitude. This last function is never used in LPD.

In LPD, we try to express from the very beginning what the protagonist might want to say (Chapter 5: 5.2). We therefore try to verbalize a language for which he lacks the words ... the sorts of things he would be happy to communicate within a group of people he knows well. We do not intrude into his personal life, and what we express is not an attempt to 'psychologize'.

Later, especially after the third day, the animators can take their lead from the protagonists. They extend the language in the sequences that protagonists propose, making particular use of synonymous expressions, and they offer corrections. The animators *never extend beyond what the protagonists want to express*, and as far as possible avoid projecting on to them their own modes of expression. This confirms the value of relational training for animators: they have to be very aware of the danger, in the double exercise, of making projections which could distort its function and effect.

The mirror

In psychodrama, the mirror technique consists of asking the protagonist to choose participants to take his or her own place in the game. This means the protagonist can watch with a certain degree of detachment and observe himself or herself through an intermediary. This new viewpoint often provokes a reaction in the protagonist.

In LPD, we use this principle in the relay technique as shown in *Dialogue without words* (Chapter 5: 5.3.1), where protagonists choose other participants to take over their roles. But, *the mirror* technique (Chapter 5: 5.2.2) used in LPD differs in form and function from the psychodramatic mirror, coming nearer to what we have known in childhood when our mother, or someone else we were fond of, repeated what we said 'in echo', and copied our miming and gestures.

Role-reversal

In LPD, we also use the psychodrama technique of role-reversal (Chapter 5: 5.3.3), in which A plays B, and vice versa. This technique appears later in LPD; it depends on a certain mastery of expression and a certain stability in relationships within the group to be able to assume someone else's role spontaneously, and to present his or her point of view in the foreign language.

Group activities

The tradition of German psychodrama has a stage which includes a series of 'protagonists' games', as well as other group activities which help participants to be more spontaneous and creative, and brings out topics which are latent in individuals or in the group as a whole. Relations between participants are expressed through an imaginary topic proposed by the participants, or by the animator according to a perception of the topics chosen by the group, e.g. cowboys, or the waiting-room in a station, or maternity ward.

My training in psychodrama has influenced my way of animating groups, and in language learning has led me to develop a type of animation which incorporates some of its characteristics. I have also transposed certain production techniques for group games or imaginary activities, in particular, the techniques for making puppets, which we will come to in Chapter 6.[5]

The ontogenetic progression of learning

Moreno compares the fundamental techniques of psychodrama, the double, the mirror, and role-reversal, to the evolutionary phases of a child.

For Moreno, the double corresponds to a 'stage of identification from *Me* to *You*, of the subject with the objects that surround him' (Moreno 1987: 169). He adds that 'one can establish a parallel between the idea of the double and the mother-child relationship before and after birth' (ibid.: 170). According to Moreno, the mirror corresponds to the 'recognition stage of the *Me* and of its uniqueness

5 We owe this activity to Erich Franzke, a German psychodramatist (Franzke 1985).

in terms of the individual' (ibid.: 169). In role-reversal, we approach what he refers to as the 'recognition stage of the *You*, the *Other*' (ibid.: 169).

After describing these three techniques, Moreno points out that they are 'rooted deeply in the dynamic strengths of human growth and can therefore be used to good effect in the treatment of mental maladies and interhuman relationships' (ibid.: 172). To which we would now add 'and in pedagogy, too!'.

These stages in our personal evolution correspond to different stages in the acquisition of our first language. This is why, during the first three days of a course, we follow an ontogenetic order of progression. We make special use of double exercises on the first day (four or five hours in an intensive course), and of mirror exercises on the second day.

Before coming on to role-reversal exercises we will have covered a number of intermediate steps, including *the triadic relationship*, and *deferred* and *direct encounter*. These stages serve no purpose in psychodrama but are necessary in LPD because they represent a progression in line with experiments carried out in acquiring our mother tongue, and symbolize different stages in communication. It is only after the second week, when we work on the idea of role and characters that we introduce the *role-reversal* technique (Chapter 5: 5.3.3 and Chapter 6).

The technique introduced on the third day is *the triadic relationship*. This is derived from a psychodramatic technique called the 'ambivalent double' which is generally used in psychodrama when someone finds it difficult to take decisions. We give it a quite different function in psychodramaturgy, and will return to this subject in Chapter 6: 6.2.3.

By adopting and adapting these techniques in the area of language learning, we can reactivate both the potential for creativity and those deep-seated sources of energy which were first present when we began to acquire our mother tongue.

1.5.2   Sources of dramaturgy

To avoid possible misunderstandings, it is important to make absolutely clear that the term 'dramaturgy' is not used to mean 'theatrical'. It is not the making of theatre, i.e. with participants putting on a show in front of other people. It involves the use of principles which make drama work and techniques derived from the stage, including actor-training, and adapting them to language learning.

Dramaturgic setting

From the very beginning, the main exercises in LPD are based on putting into action dramaturgic functions (Souriau 1950). Of six functions described by Souriau we have kept three which seem to us to be essential in pedagogy. We have given them psychological denominations adapted to our work: *desire, opposition,* and *support.* If one person has a wish or project and someone else opposes it, a dramaturgic action will result from the opposing forces. Depending on the circumstances, the other participants will support one side or the other, and so modify the direction and balance of the action.

Reference must also be made to the principle of *resonance.* Tragedy in classical theatre involved its audience because its themes concerned them directly or symbolically; the exercises and topics in LPD observe this principle of resonance. After the third week, or earlier with more advanced language participants, we employ these criteria when we select and work with written texts, which in due course may lead on to dramaturgization (Chapter 7).

During the second week, participants are transported into the world of the imagination. To put the group's topics into action we refer as much to psychodramatic as to dramatic traditions. Participants take on social, imaginary, or mythical roles which allow them to activate other aspects of themselves, and to adopt new behaviours. The imagination not only enlarges the real world, but leads the group into other dimensions which themselves release new energies. Assuming a new character encourages them to express themselves.

At this point we also use scene-setting techniques derived from dramaturgical situations, and elements of Sheleen's work, as well as her exercises in space-time (Sheleen 1983; Dropsy 1973).

'Return to the exterior reality' is a phase which marks the end of a long introductory stage, when we use the dramatization techniques referred to in Chapter 5: 5.4, including some of those described in Augusto Boal's *Théâtre-Forum* (Boal 1980a, 1983).

The function of the masks

In LPD, we use four sorts of masks: 'whole' masks, in which participants cannot see or speak; 'blind' half masks which allow the wearer to speak but not see; 'seeing' masks which are half masks with eye holes in which wearers can speak and hear, and finally 'mouth' half masks in which they can see but not speak. We shall return to the use of these masks in Chapter 5: 5.2.1.

First and foremost, masks have a protective function. Whole and blind half masks protect wearers from the other participants, who are sometimes felt to be just observers. Being observed can have an inhibiting, even a paralysing effect. At the same time, the masks allow the protagonist to concentrate on himself or herself. They facilitate a return to oneself and sometimes perhaps to the original in oneself; they increase a readiness to listen as well as feelings of openness. The protagonist perceives his or her own voice and the voice of the animator in double, more clearly, so that a nuance can be appreciated. The masks also have a soothing function, resulting in a calm which encourages concentration and receptivity.

We believe that wearing masks helps improve retention because they intensify concentration. In Greek antiquity, the *aedes* who were charged with learning the traditional writings by heart were blind: perhaps it is easier to memorize the language with the eyes closed.

The alienating effect of masks allows for a new learning context in which participants can develop a different attitude towards learning a foreign language and finding a new creative space. Participants can feel different, behave differently, enter into contact with other aspects of themselves, let other modes of expression appear, use new relational structures, and thus broaden their identity.

Masks also have a symbolic function. Their ritual character means that they are able to convey a mythological signification. The whole mask, for instance, can symbolize the initiation of death which opens the way to a new birth in the foreign language. These whole masks, which are used only once by each participant on the first day of the course, also reinforce the symbolic functions of the double, mirror, and role-reversal used in the three first three days of a course.

Masks are used at a stage when protagonists who do not have the linguistic self-sufficiency to express themselves directly, are still dependant on the language offered to them by the animator. As participants take more responsibility for what they say, the masks become less necessary; their use relates to the linguistic evolution of the participants.

1.6 Conclusion

LPD is an approach rather than a method, conveyed by a sensitive conception of mankind and language acquisition. As Moreno wrote:

> At present the pupil is usually treated like a frog whose cerebral cortex has been removed. He is allowed to reproduce only roles

which are conserved. The reproductive process of learning must move into second place; first emphasis should be given to the productive, spontaneous-creative process of learning. The exercise and training of spontaneity is the chief subject of the school of the future. (Moreno 1973: 81)

For those of us using LPD, this future Moreno has talked about has already begun.

2 The methodological foundations of linguistic psychodramaturgy

In some respects the methodological hypotheses on which linguistic psychodramaturgy (LPD) is based are very different from those of traditional teaching. We shall, therefore, begin by introducing aspects of our approach to the foreign language, and contrasting these with some traditional concepts.

2.1 The functions of language

Language is the mother, not the servant, of thought. [KRAUS]

Whenever we set out to teach something we should keep in mind the characteristics of our objectives. In the case of foreign language teaching this means the functions of language, and how far we take them into account in the learning process.

We cannot think of acquiring a foreign language in the same way as, say, a scientific fact because our first language plays such a vital role in our lives, contributing to the development of our physical, affective, intellectual, social, and spiritual life. Hence, Lacan's perceptive description of a person as 'the speaking being' (parlêtre) (Lacan 1966). Speech is the expression of that being, it is the language of understanding reality, and expressing what we imagine. Speech is marked in a personal and individualized way, physically, emotionally, and intellectually, by our past. Talking implies more than using words within a structural framework; it encompasses habits of expression and relationship, interactive procedures, and types of social functioning which cannot be neglected or ignored when designing a language learning method.

Teaching any language is not the same as teaching a subject such as mathematics; learning a language cannot be restricted to the accumulation of knowledge within a particular framework.

Acquiring our first language has left such a strong mark on our personalities that we underestimate at our peril the impact a language, even a foreign one, can have on the individual. It influences both how we relate and how we communicate, and so we must take into account all the effects of the language we are teaching.

Let us consider then what essential functions, beyond the purely linguistic functions, language fulfils for each of us, since some are integral to all language and must therefore be taken into account when we learn a foreign language.

2.1.1   The symbolic function

The symbolic function of language is an essential reason for using our first language. It allows us to summon up what seems to be miss-ing and, symbolically, to represent it. Freud illustrates this symbolism in the game of an eighteen month-old child who amuses himself playing with a wooden bobbin on a string. Here is an extract:

> ... still holding on to the string he threw the bobbin very precisely over the edge of his bed, which had a curtain around it, where it disappeared. Then he made his invariable o-o-o-o sound and pulled the bobbin back onto the bed, this time greeting it with a joyous 'Da!' (There!). (Freud 1951: 16)

Freud offers the following interpretation:

> The child disengaged himself, as it were, from the harm of his mother's departure, and from her absence, by reproducing, with the objects he had to hand, the scene of her disappearance and reappearance. (Freud 1951: 17)

Here, we are witnessing play and language joined together in their symbolic function: in the example given, the game and the statement help to sublimate and control reality.

This symbolic function is not only essential to the development of the individual's emotional life; it is also a fundamental characteristic of all expression through language. This is why it is important to include it in any approach to a foreign language, and it is strongly represented in LPD, as we shall find in Chapters 5 and 6.

2.1.2   The expressive function

Before becoming a medium for developing and sustaining relation-ships, language is primarily a medium for expression. Language allows us to 'tell ourselves about ourselves' before 'telling about ourselves to others'. Every communication contains an element of self-expression, and listening to oneself is at the heart of all successful communication. Thanks to language, we can express what we feel, experience, and think.

Talking helps us to encounter sensations, emotions, feelings, thoughts, impressions, and images which are often latent within us, of which we may not be consciously aware. So, language has an exploratory function, helping us to encounter that which dwells in our subconscious. In talking, we go beyond what we consciously know and bring to the surface thoughts and memories we may never have consciously perceived; new connections are made in the unconscious networks of our inner emotional and intellectual life. An act of expressing ourselves can allow us to perceive our inner lives more clearly, and discover how we feel in relation to that experience. Speech, then, is at any one time both social and individual.

Speech is not just an expression of a conscious, previously conceptualized, thought. But we are often led to believe this in traditional teaching, which assumes a three-stage pattern for expression: conceptualization–formulization–articulation.

Speech is also not just a means of clarification; it permits an extension of our thinking. Thought develops as it is expressed; therefore, language carries out a creative function. It is not only an expression of oneself and a means of finding oneself, it is an extension of oneself.

Because language has these vital exploratory and creative functions, it follows that it is fundamental to offer participants a pedagogy which makes them want to express themselves, for it is by expressing themselves that they really communicate. This personalization of the foreign language assists appropriation and retention.

In traditional teaching, the expressive function is all too often relegated to what is called the 'transfer' stage at the end of the course. And when this is linked to a requirement simply to practise words and structures studied in class, this stage turns out to be artifical and over-controlled.

LPD concentrates on the expressive function in the first three days and then throughout the course because it seems to us that, before coming into contact with other people, the participant should be brought into contact with the self in the foreign language.

In the double and mirror stage, and when we are staging the LPD sequences (Chapter 5), we find an analogy with a situation familiar to us from our first language.

Our inner language is obviously never heard by anyone else, has no expectation of influencing an actual interlocutor. The egocentric language of the child is not concerned about an interlocutor, but it tolerates, and even looks for, the presence of a listener. (Jakobson, quoted by Richelle 1976: 126)

It is during the first three days especially that the group on an LPD course fulfils this function of the listener who provides an 'echo', by being present, sometimes in silence, as a witness and helper to the protagonist.

2.1.3   The communicative function

Speech is 'a movement towards' oneself or other people; it helps us to discover where we are in relation to others, to take our place and to find our surroundings. It contributes to our perception of others through what they say and is the primary means of communicating with them.

Valid communication is only possible if the content is not determined in advance but by the speakers themselves. Speakers must be the authors of their own words and not mere peddlers of someone else's expression.

It follows that any approach to a foreign language has to take account of this communicative function. Language cannot be reduced to a functional medium, destined to carry out speech acts according to a prepared programme, without considering the impact of the message on the individuals concerned. Talking is communication; it is not an exchange of linguistic formulae emptied of personal qualities of meaning and value. Communication involves an encounter with emotions and thoughts peculiar to each of the speakers. We must, therefore, be careful to offer participants types of communication which take this into account.

2.1.4   The structuring function

Talking plays a central role in the understanding and structuring of our minds, our real and imaginary worlds; it helps us to extend our control over our interior world and the world outside. Vygotsky (1964) observes that children of four or five years verbalize complex situations with which they are faced in order to control them more effectively. Naming things, defining situations verbally, leads the way to better control over them.

Language not only allows us to perceive and structure the world as it is but also to transform reality, showing it in a different light and from a new perspective. As we speak we are constructing our world.

It is, therefore, important to stimulate intellectual curiosity, the participants' spirit of discovery, in the foreign language. Facilitating their perception of alternative forms of language structure, of alternative ways of looking at the world, develops their mental faculties, which in turn helps towards a better control of their surroundings.

Conclusion

In LPD, we give special importance to these four functions of the language. In the first few days we concentrate on the *expressive function*, and move gradually towards a development of the *communicative function*. The *symbolic function* continually accompanies the acquisition process according to the type of exercises carried out (Chapters 5 and 6). We take account of the *structuring function* by suggesting exercises to participants in which their intellectual capacities can continue to develop.

2.2 The relationship between the first language and a foreign language

Language teachers often think of the first language as a source of linguistic interference, a source of errors in the foreign language. They consider language in essentially lexical or structural terms. But the relationships between the first language and foreign languages can be observed at a deeper level.

When we begin to learn another language we are not blank sheets of paper: the words we use are carriers of our past, and continue to be weighed down by their history. They bear the marks of the relationships and situations in which we first encountered them, as well as the subjective imprint of their origin or of their use in our linguistic life. Their meaning is reactivated more, or less, in relation to a particular context.

To speak another language requires a physical transformation of how we talk, our body rhythm, and our way of breathing. It also calls for a different structuring of thought and of the world, another perception, another understanding of the world of the speaker of the foreign language. To enter a foreign language is to enter a foreign world.

A person's general attitude towards the unknown, the strange and the foreign is revealed when learning a foreign language. For some, the response may be curiosity, interest in the new, and the desire to experiment; others will be anxious about being lost in an unknown world; for others the foreign language can represent a form of aggression and become synonymous with risk or danger. This is why it is important to provide participants with a reassuring framework so that they can feel confident enough to 'take a chance' in the foreign language.

Learning a foreign language can also awaken profound identity problems, particularly those to do with nationality. If I speak German 'like a German' I might be taken for a German, I might be mistaken for someone else. These inhibitions are often strengthened by conscious and subconscious connotations.

A language is often identified with our image of those, including the teacher, who speak it. It can appear pleasant, difficult, or repulsive. In addition, the teacher unconsciously conveys a personal relationship with the language and with those who speak it. The world of the foreign language is therefore a personal, even mythical, one and often one in which it is difficult to feel comfortable.

The foreign language may, however, provide the possibility to experiment in new forms of expression. In a new language we can try fresh experiences, behave differently, experience attitudes and reactions we never dared to adopt in our first language. We can, for example, restore flexibility to rigid behaviour patterns. The foreign language can also act like a mask, allowing us to behave as another person while remaining ourselves. And our first language may be associated with a world of repressive education, so that acquiring a foreign language in a sensitive framework makes it possible to begin a new form of self-expression.

At times the acquisition of another language allows some participants to distance themselves from the world of their mother tongue. They are given a new opportunity for self-expression. I recall a participant in psychodrama who at times of strong emotion preferred to express himself in English rather than in his first language, which I also spoke, because English was his language and not his father's! Yet again, a participant told us during the second week of an intensive LPD course that she was delighted not to have stammered at all in French since the course began. Her stammering did not recur except once very briefly, and she still has it under control.

As well as opening the way into a foreign culture and to meeting foreigners, the new language can be a doorway opening on to another perception of oneself and one's inner life; this other perception can bring me nearer to defining who I am. The 'other' highlights my particular way of being and has the function of a mirror.

Contact with a foreign language can also encourage awareness, respect, and acceptance of other people. It can help mutual understanding, not just between people of different nationalities but in one's relations with other people generally. It can awaken a healthy curiosity for what is different, and develop an attitude of openness towards the foreign and the unknown.

All this means that the approach to the foreign language must give participants a feeling of confidence so that they can be both themselves and, simultaneously, 'other' in that language. The *double, mirror*, and *triadic relationships* (Chapter 5) symbolize the relationships experienced when we acquired our first language, and allow an empathetic contact with the foreign language to be established. The same exercises encourage an acceptance of other people as they are, with all their strengths, weaknesses, limitations, fears, and hopes.

2.3 LPD's approach to the foreign language

Language ... conveys a specific experience and the teacher must maintain the connection between language and experience.
[DE AJURIAGUERRA 1977: 346]

In traditional teaching the language is, for the most part, conveyed through the medium of a textbook. The contents of the book will determine what the students learn and very largely how they learn. We could say that this sort of teaching involves an indirect approach to the language because, generally speaking, a book comes between the students and the language.

In LPD, the language is created on the spot. It comes directly from the participants in the first week or, later on, through outline activities or topics related to the life of the group involved. In this way, the language is experienced directly.

2.3.1 Sequence technique

Many creative techniques can give rise to problems when they are transposed to a linear form of foreign language learning. Participants talk, talk, talk, but do not experience useful variations in the language which could help them to broaden and strengthen their expression. The *sequence* technique we use continuously in LPD helps us avoid this problem and to have contact with language which, instead of having a linear pattern, recurs in a 'progressive spiral', within which the content can be repeated and reformulated with variations:

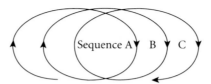

FIGURE 6 *Development of a sequence*

Thus, during the first two days (Chapter 5: 5.2) when the animator is creating a sequence, he or she tries to 'juggle' with words while giving the sequence a certain rhythm. The animator plays with alternates or opposites in order to reinforce the rhythmical, musical, and at times, poetical character of the sequence, and draws on images and metaphors, visual and auditory sensations, taste, touch, smell, in order to awaken all the senses. All of this happens within a spiral which is continually bringing back variations of the content of the sequence in a new order.

This technique for building the sequence encourages not only a development of content but also a significant amount of work on the form of the language. By way of illustration, here is how the first version of two sequences develops.[1]

Here is the first sequence:

> It is sweet, calm, melodious. It flows like a stream, left, right, sweetly, slowly, tenderly. It comes and goes like a spring, and I go forward sweetly, calmly ... I go forward in my own rhythm, sometimes slow, sometimes fast, like a stream which goes, comes, which flows, which leaps, calm or full of joy. And I go on, from here to there, here ... at my own rhythm, sometimes slow, sometimes fast ...

Here is another sequence, with another participant:

> I am there and I am waiting for this little journey, a fine little journey, a beautiful little journey, pleasant, quiet, no worries, no problems. A little journey for me, only for me. Not too far. No, not too far, but really quiet, pleasant. And now I'm going. I am going on a little journey. Slowly at first, that's it, we're going, a little journey to a nice place, no worries, no problems. Where? I don't know, I don't know yet, we'll see. It's coming, it'll work out. A little journey, not too long, not too far, a really pleasant little journey ... a quiet journey, marvellous ...

The sequence is repeated several times, evolving in relation to the echo from the participant wearing the half mask. In this way, he or she gradually gains confidence in the language according to personal wishes and capacities for expression.

1 These sequences (translated) were spontaneously created by Marie, my wife, in double, on the first day of an LPD French course with a group composed of complete beginners and false-beginners.

We have illustrated the creation and development of the sequence in a double exercise, the sort used on the first day of an LPD course, in which the sequence is spontaneously created by the animator. Sequences and dialogues created later in the course by the participants themselves will be extended and enriched in the same way (Chapters 5 and 6). A change in the structure of the exercise, or a change of partners, will enable participants to make a fresh approach to the situation. That will, in turn, lead to variations or developments of the content of their expression, while retaining a reassuring core of familiar language. The verbal sequence expands like the movements of a juggler who repeats the same routine a number of times before starting to introduce variations, or an entirely new routine which is gradually perfected.

The variations within the repetition, and the continuity within the changes, mean that the sequence develops in accordance with the principles of displacement and condensation. That is to say, it sometimes evolves like a spiral rotating around its centre, then moves laterally. Or, it can concentrate on a particular area, looking at it from different angles while continuing to consolidate basic knowledge of the language with the help of synonyms.

Some sequences resemble a sonata in which a theme carried by a rhythm is gradually revealed; variations begin to appear, or the melody suddenly diverts to a new path. In the same way, the developing sequence does not go off in every direction as it develops, but preserves its internal structure. This encourages organic progress in the foreign language.

The sequence demands spontaneity and mastery on the part of the animators, whether they are creating the sequence themselves or working in double to help participants enlarge and enrich their verbal expression. It is not something to entrust to the unskilled practitioner.

2.3.2 Content

The content is not determined in advance; the language springs up naturally in the here and now. Speech is born out of the need for expression arising from the situation within the group, so what is spoken by participants belongs to them, an expression of their own individuality.

The topics and content vary according to the participants and the group but it can be said that the language retains a certain unity and that the linguistic content intersects; it is the language of the inner being and its relationship to the outside world, the language of sensations, feelings, emotions, the expression of needs and desires, observations, intentions, inter-personal relations, etc.—a *relational language*, which brings together the real and the imaginary, and on to which a functional language can be grafted according to need. What participants chiefly acquire, therefore, is the capacity to express themselves in the foreign language.

2.3.3   Progression

All linguistic acquisition is essentially individual. Each participant progresses according to individual aptitudes and interests, previous linguistic experience, and the point of personal and linguistic evolution reached. At the end of the first lesson, even complete beginners do not share the same knowledge, unless the content has been deliberately held back to ensure that everyone has the same level of acquired knowledge. Instead of deluding ourselves with illusions of an effective linguistic or functional progression, it is better to help the participant mark out a personal path in the language, and offer a language that is as varied as possible so that each can respond to it according to his or her personal 'resonance'. In this way, the participant draws from the language according to his or her own receptivity, sensibility, needs, desires, and linguistic maturity.

Stage one

Animators take their lead from the participants. In LPD, the criteria for progression are, above all, relational. During the first three days of an intensive course we focus on each participant using the *double, mirror,* and *triadic relationship* exercises (Chapter 5), trying to adapt ourselves to each person's rhythm and needs. From the fourth day, participants leave the symbolic world of the primary group in which they have already begun to establish their position and to define themselves. This has been a protective environment in which their interlocutors, the animators, adapted their own behaviour to support them. In the next stages they meet first one, then gradually all, the other members of the group.

The relationship with the language begins with activities which encourage a turning-in on oneself, a return to the sources of our verbal selves, to the roots of our expression, to the imaginary and symbolic world we live in from our earliest years. The participant moves outwards then from an inner self before progressing towards individuals or the group as a whole. In this way, we set in motion a movement from the interior towards the exterior, from impression towards expression. We witness a gradual transition from the 'I' to the 'you'. There is an evolution from an essentially egocentric language towards a socialized language.

During the second week this progression evolves by a symbolic rediscovery of the history of mankind. We return, little by little, to the sources of our imaginary world.

We start by using techniques which refer to our contemporary world, such as *social roles*, techniques using characters in photos, for example (Chapter 5: 3.3). We now have socially-marked characters who are close to our conscious world, sometimes accompanied by stereotypes which help the approach.

We then move on to roles performed by fictional characters, which we could call *fairy-tale roles*. These characters enable us to penetrate that magical world of childhood.

Finally, with *mythical roles*, we arrive in a world nearer to our unconscious instincts, a world which reflects the origins of our imaginations, and which expresses itself through archetypes (Chapter 6). This cycle ends with a return to external reality, which prepares participants for meeting another world outside the classroom (Chapter 5: 5.6).

Stage two

In stage two of the learning process, from the third week, participants can choose between two paths: one is aimed at broadening and deepening their general knowledge of the language, mainly using topics and techniques which activate the imagination; the other includes those with specialist needs (for people in industry, for example), involving more functional work on specific professional situations employing a variety of LPD techniques such as doubling, role-play, etc. (Chapters 5 and 6).

We also develop a spiral progression which gradually includes the individual, social, and universal spheres (Figure 7). It should be understood that all three spheres are involved throughout, though some are emphasized more than others in particular exercises.

In the first week we begin with communication exercises which engage the here and now of participants; in the second week we introduce outline activities which seem to us to correspond to the emotional development of the group but which transpose the topics into a more imaginary world. This enlarges the expressive field, opening up a new, intensely symbolic dimension with consequently a new significance for the participants' expression. They are closer to themselves in their imagination than if they were reproducing situations from textbooks. The techniques we use reinforce the connection between the speakers and the language used to express themselves.

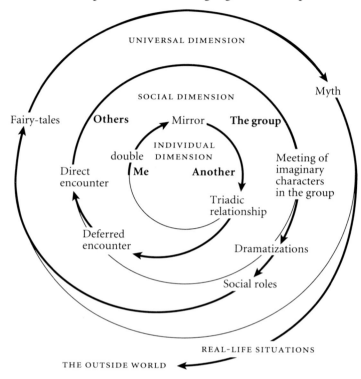

FIGURE 7 *Spiral evolution in LPD*

There must also be a progression in the linguistic support given to participants by the animators. During the first two days, the animators present the language directly to the participants. Little by little this role transforms itself as the group makes progress in its knowledge of the language. When a participant and the group cannot find adequate expression, the animators, in double, give whatever linguistic support is needed, or enlarge the vocabulary used by the participants by providing them with synonymous expressions. The animators include a corrective function as the participants develop their skills, and provide the exact expression when participants offer an incorrect formulation. As the participants acquire confidence in the language, more emphasis is given to the two functions of enlarging and correcting the language progress. Other types of progression also occur in some of the exercises, involving gesture, utterances and verbal progression (Chapters 4, 5, and 6).

Finally, it is worth noting that the use of masks is also progressive.

The full mask, for example, is used only in the first double exercise, and the others are gradually abandoned as participants become able to express themselves more independently.

2.3.4 Understanding language structure

We all know that students do not learn a rule because we teach it to them, and the fact that they have learnt a rule does not mean they will apply it. Much could be said about the way rules are explained, how they are formulated, how they might be transferred. In trying to anticipate grammatical problems we so often create them.

It would be interesting to know what impact an approach which focuses on grammatical correctness has on the spontaneity of expression of students. Fear of grammatical errors sometimes leads learners in traditional courses to express themselves in 'grammatically faultless silence'. It would be equally interesting to know what mental functions 'cognitive' methods relate to, and how far they contribute to the intellectual development of the learners. Clearly, a programmed learning of grammar leaves open numerous questions about its efficacy. How does LPD differ?

The first point to make is that, since LPD courses are intensive, the grammatical problems are not the same as in extensive courses. Participants are exposed to the structures of the language intensively and in a particular way; this encourages the conscious and unconscious generalization of use, i.e. an intuitive awareness of grammatical phenomena associated with the foreign language, and an inductive production with grammatical rules.

So we can observe both the subconscious creation and conscious discovery of those rules which control the construction of the foreign language. This is helped by the intensity of the courses, which increases the frequency of contact with language. The capacity for classification, for abstract thought, generalization, transfers by analogy, and creation of hypotheses and rules becomes much easier because the structure is lived, experienced, and discovered in action. In LPD grammar is not separated from language in context.

We do not plan grammatical activities in precise detail because language is discovered in responding to the needs and expressions of the participants. Moreover, we give expression priority over correctness—expression first, correct expression second—but this does not mean that we encourage participants to be careless or lazy in their use of the language.

When a participant formulates an incorrect expression the

animators act as doubles to reformulate what was said, especially
during the initial 'setting-up' phase of the sequence. The amount of
corrective intervention in the first days varies according to how
confident the participant feels using the language, and increases
gradually as the course continues. Our approach is always to offer
an 'improved' formulation or version of what was said and not to
impose the 'correct' version. Depending on what personal targets a
protagonist has, he or she will either pay attention to what is said and
adopt the suggestions offered or carry on as before. We let each participant take personal responsibility for the quality of their expression.

Attitudes to the quality of the language used often vary according
to the commitment of participants during the exercise. Sometimes
they are so involved in the activity that they want to communicate
their message above all else, and pay little attention to what form it
takes: the protagonist presses on without appearing to have noticed
the corrections offered. But these corrections may have been perceived consciously or unconsciously by them, or by other members
of the group, and so bear fruit at a later date. We have often noticed
that attitudes to correction go through several stages. The initial wish
to express oneself in the foreign language is soon followed by the
wish to communicate in a more precise, more varied, and more
linguistically correct way. Self-correction and correction by the
group become more frequent as the course develops.

I remember an LPD weekend where, after an intensive two-week
course, we were working with stories and on the second day of the
course the animators frequently had to correct the expression 'Je
crois *que* ...', 'Je pense *que* ...'. After some time all but one participant had understood and was able to use *que* correctly. After a while,
whenever he began a sentence containing a verb of opinion, the
group chorused *que* in a friendly way, then waited expectantly. As
a result, to everyone's satisfaction, he took special care to use *que*
correctly.

Also, we have often noticed the phenomenon of increased correction in the group as a whole without being able to explain it. I
remember one course in particular where, on the Thursday of the
second week, I could feel that the group's skills had improved notice-
ably from the previous evening. This phenomenon is often observed
when one course follows another after a break of a few weeks, as if
the brain had accumulated a lot of information and structured it in
the interval. Participants were more advanced than at the end of the
previous course even though no language work had been undertaken
in the interval.

Grammar rules are no longer emphasized before the act of speaking but are discovered by the group in the context of problems they encounter. Correctness is attached to usage instead of preceding it. Error is productive because, when identified in context, it leads to a meaningful awareness of correct structure. Participants discover the rules which determine a phenomenon for themselves. What is more they develop discovery strategies which are often more important than the rule obtained. Importantly, the rule relates to their level of knowledge at the time the problem arises, and does not refer to the level of a teacher's more complete grammatical knowledge.

Spontaneous explanations given by other participants sometimes have an economy and an impact which we may not have as teachers. For example, during a session learning French, a participant had used the adverb *trop* (*too*) and when the animator corrected her sentence with *très* (*very*) she indicated that she could not understand the difference. Another participant gave her this reply: '*Très, c'est bien. Trop, c'est mal!*' ('*Very is good. Too is bad!*'). In the circumstances of the activity this explanation was sufficient.

We take a more analytical approach to language in the third or fourth week of an LPD course, particularly where written activities are concerned, using explanations of the functioning of the language or using relevant themes which encompass a broad range of information. When there is a request for a grammatical problem to be clarified, or an error is repeated which could be avoided by a conscious understanding of the relevant grammatical point, we propose a discovery of the rule using errors made by the group. To do this, we use the technique of conceptualization described by Besse (1974). This means that the animators have a role, where necessary, in giving structure to the discovery process (Dufeu 1982). In a traditional concept of learning, error is seen as a delay or obstacle in relation to the targeted result.

In our pedagogy, error is an indispensable means of experiencing the characteristics, possibilities, and limitations of the foreign language. This experiential view of language learning helps towards an acceptance of error as an integral part of learning. Some participants are astonished by how patient animators can be when participants make mistakes; animators have to repeat the same correct formula several times. I do not think it is a question of patience so much as an attitude to acquisition and error, above all towards the participant, who is accepted with his or her limitations and is considered to be in a state of constant evolution.

2.3.5 Conclusions

Our grammatical approach is based on the following hypotheses:

- There is no division between grammar and language. By expressing themselves, participants come into contact with the structures of the language and acquire them.
- Grammar follows error and develops in relation to it. Grammar is not preventive so is not inhibiting. People understand and retain better what they discover and formulate for themselves.
- Exercises which let the participants build up the rule in context develop an attitude of investigation, discovery, and experimentation. To encourage research is pedagogically more important than to offer a prepared response because it leads to increased awareness.
- Each structure that is learnt is transitory because it is constantly developing, changing, maturing. Grammatical knowledge is also in a constant state of being built, broadened, and modified in relation to the stage of language acquisition. There is no concept of an end: knowledge of a language is a process of constant and perpetual evolution.
- Every grammatical rule is made to be forgotten. What is important is to apply it; to formulate a rule is only a step to controlling the structure.
- Language acquisition is essentially a personal process; linguistic maturity from understanding grammatical phenomena varies from one individual to another: one participant will be receptive at a given moment while another will take longer.

2.4 Comprehension in the communicative process

Sense comes from context as much as from the text. [GINGER 1987]

Before examining the comprehension processes in LPD it may help to begin with some observations about the act of understanding.

We never understand everything, but we always understand something; very often we understand something else. We are condemned to mistakes and misunderstandings which are sometimes so small that we are not even aware of them. And, understanding is not just a conscious or intellectual activity. When I say 'I understand you' I am not merely expressing the result of an intellectual operation; I am stating that my emotional self is in resonance with the other person. Understanding presupposes an act of acceptance of the other person and a close, even if momentary, relationship with that other person.

Even when we understand the words used it does not mean that we understand the message in the statement. Our comprehension is a function of various perceptions: our referential world; our perceptional habits, our needs, and our expectations. That is why we sometimes hear only what we expect to hear. Often, when I think I have understood something, it turns out that I have failed to *listen*. Each time we listen to other people we have to remember that we understand them through ourselves. Sometimes I must listen to myself first to know what I am hearing. Understanding, in other words, depends on how we listen to ourselves as well as to others, just as, in our first language, we sometimes repeat what someone has said to us in order to grasp it more readily.

At this point, it may help to clarify the distinction between *propositional* and *illocutionary meaning* with the help of a few examples. The sense of 'It is ten o'clock.' is that the tenth hour of the day has just begun—it marks a moment in time. The meaning of this statement depends on its context. And it reflects the relationship between the speakers. It is transmitted by gesture, tone, and other paralinguistic signals. It can mean 'You are early (or late)', 'I am impatient', 'At last I can go', etc. When a mother says 'I love you!' to her child, the child perceives the particular meaning and grasps the sense of the word 'love', through the situation, the mother's gesture and tone, and experience of the relationship with her. The child *feels* what is expressed. He or she understands the meaning by experiencing it and perception is reinforced through intellectual processes. As adults, we continue the same process of understanding, but sometimes we have to re-establish contact with it.

The illocutionary force of a message stems not only from the explicit sense of the words, but from its context—the relationship between the speakers, their roles, what they hope to achieve through the message. It also depends on their language comprehension models and their paralinguistic perceptions, including gestures, miming, and physical attitudes. The distance between the two speakers can also be important. Meaning is also conveyed by rhythm, intonation, and tone of voice. It includes all the connotations carried by the message.

It is only by taking all these elements into account that the words become meaningful. Context directs the sense of the words towards an understanding of the meaning. When, in a dialogue between Jane Birkin and Serge Gainsbourg, one says *'I love you!'* and the other replies *'I don't either'* the latter has understood the significance of the

speaker's statement, and reacts not to what is said but to what has
been expressed.

Understanding comes not only from factual information but, due
to the imagination which surrounds the facts, from the reverbera-
tions the statement produces in us, and intuitive communication
from subconscious to subconscious. Understanding brings together
reason and intuition. We cannot use language as if it had no particular meaning for the speaker and the listener, since 'Before language
has meaning, it means something to someone' (Lacan 1966: 82). In
other words, to understand a message fully implies grasping the
meaning given to it by the speaker, because language is relational and
that is what communication is.

So, we should not stop at the explicit sense of words, we must also
take into account their connotative values. We cannot reduce words
to a single interpretation, as some teaching approaches tend to do.
We have to avoid separating sense from meaning; what we *say* from
what we *express*.

2.4.1   Comprehension in LPD

In LPD, comprehension finds its position fundamentally reversed
when compared with what happens in most traditional teaching.
Most of all, it is up to the animators to understand the participants
and then provide them with the means to express themselves, not the
reverse. It seems logical that the person with the better knowledge of
the language should try to grasp what someone who is learning it
wants to express. So, the animator has to be alert to what participants
wish to express.

Understanding rests, in part, on the empathetic relationship which
the animators establish with participants: they have to try to get on
the same wavelength as the participants and become aware of what
they need and want to express. Only when this has been achieved will
they be able to provide the linguistic material needed by the participants. The act of comprehension is directed towards the person rather
than the language.

Understanding also stems from the close relationship between the
language and the situation experienced in LPD. Since the language
derives from the participants, it is rich in connotations. The language
originates in the participants, drawing from their reality and their
imagination, and the situation experienced directly in the here and
now: understanding the meaning of the message is easier because the
participants are experiencing its context.

Our approach in LPD is not primarily directed towards perceptions of propositional meaning. We start by inviting participants to enter into the rhythms, melody, and sounds of the language. Letting the language enter into them rhythmically and melodically before trying to grasp meaning helps their understanding, which comes from within themselves (Chapters 4 and 5).

Approaching language in this way encourages participants to develop an intuitive perception of meaning through experience of a message with its particular nuances and through the feelings evoked by its tones and sounds. This always accompanies intellectual understanding. Consider the meaning to each individual of a period of silence, a musical work, or an abstract picture. It includes opening one's mind to an interpretation rather than looking for meaning outside oneself. Using various relaxation, breathing, and other exercises can extend further this open attitude.

We encourage participants to let meaning emerge rather than to try too hard to find it; to take risks in understanding. How a participant's interlocutor responds will confirm or contradict their hypotheses. They know they have the right not to understand or even to understand something else. As we have seen, appropriate understanding comes from a combination of situation, context, and paralinguistic elements. By doing all this, especially in the double and mirror exercises of the first few days, we encounter language through a strongly intuitive form of communication—what Dolto (1985) has called 'pre-semantic comprehension'. The approach to sense and meaning, then, is sensitive and intuitive as well as intellectual.

With the exception of the first two days, when the content of the sequence is provided by the animator, a wider range of expression is grafted on to the participant's utterances. The double provides different ways of expressing what he or she says, and in so doing increases the power of expression. The development of the sequence in LPD involves focusing on synonyms, a broadening by analogy of the means of expression, so that participants can gradually enrich their expression using deduction and association. Comprehension broadens as language skills increase. On other occasions, comprehension grows in a mosaic pattern; because they understand the context, participants are able to decode unfamiliar words and phrases: they broaden their vocabulary by deduction, making connections between fragments.

A sequence is repeated several times with some variations. This provides the opportunity to understand progressively the particular meaning of a message, including wild guesses as well as logical hypotheses. Meaning percolates through little by little with the help of minor changes and corrections from animators or other participants. Comprehension is a continuous and living process.

Comprehension can also take place more straightforwardly because of the similarity between words in the first language and the foreign language. In LPD, participants can often manage to give an approximate version of what they want to express using words from their first language. For example, a beginner might say '*I speak little little English*' and the animator might respond with '*I speak very little English*'. The animator, in empathetic relationship with the protagonist, sees that he or she wants to express something and provides linguistic help by repeating the expression with the linguistic material needed. In this way, knowledge is increased by way of sensitive and flexible sequencing.

2.4.2   Conclusions

In LPD, comprehension is encouraged in several ways:

— After the first two stages content is determined by participants. As a result, the language learnt is based on what they want/need to express and their experiences. It comes from themselves and is expanded according to their needs.

— Since the participant is the author of his or her language during the sessions, a direct and strong bond is created between the speaker and the language used.

— The meaning of statements has a strong contextual value because activities are centred on the participants' here and now; there is a balance between the situation and the language.

— The empathetic relationships which develop in groups, and the types of interaction LPD encourages, give rise to what might be called a shared or co-experienced encounter. This encourages a deeper understanding, which captures the essential meaning of a message.

— Small groups, and the types of exercises used, help develop the identification with other members of the group and develop our empathetic comprehension.

— Participants are totally immersed in the learning experience; their intellect, emotions, and bodies are involved in the communication process; thoughts, emotions, and sensations take part in the perception and interpretation of the language. Understanding is not, therefore, the result of using one's intellect, but an activity of the whole being.

- In LPD, the target language is experienced in all its poetic and
  symbolic richness; this also helps towards an intuitive comprehension of the message.
- In LPD activities, participants become familiar with a broad use of
  the language. This can help them to capture meaning by experiencing unfamiliar linguistic elements; they may develop new
  perceptions and decoding strategies.
- There are numerous exercises to reinforce concentration and
  attentive listening.
- Careful listening is developed, for example, using masks during
  the first three days and using exercises which enhance the rhythmic and melodic characteristics of the foreign language.
- Openness and receptivity are encouraged by a general atmosphere
  in the sessions which reinforces confidence and a willingness to
  experiment, all of which helps comprehension.
- Experimentation also encourages participants to hypothesize or
  guess, to want to discover whatever is strange and unknown.
- Traditional relationships to comprehension are reversed: it is
  mainly up to the animators, who speak the language well, to
  understand what the participants want to express, not the
  reverse.

2.5 Retention

It seems necessary for us to make the distinction between memorizing and retention. Retention involves keeping and refining facts in
the memory, while memorizing is commiting something to one's
memory; it is a voluntary act which can end in retention, for example, when we repeat the same activity several times. But we do not
always need to memorize something in order to retain it (e.g. in the
case of advertisements). Most of what we know, including most of
our memories and range of knowledge, has never been deliberately
memorized; it has been directly retained for a variety of reasons.

To explain retention, think of a situation in which you have
instantly retained a word or an expression heard only once in the
foreign language. Consider the criteria which help you to understand why you retained that particular word or expression after only
one hearing. For example, you may have retained the word or
expression because it produced an 'affective echo' in you, perhaps
due to its context, a personal interest in the subject or situation, the
phonic resonance, its resemblance to a word in your first language, a
mental image because of its associations, or the coincidence between

discovering a word or experience and needing to use it, even because you had a special forceful need for the item at the time. Various other factors have important roles to play, including your strength of contact with the language, your attitude to the new and foreign, your linguistic curiosity, openness, etc.

LPD does not use memorizing techniques to effect retention. Although the terms and structures which occur in sequence exercises may be repeated several times, the objective of these repetitions is not memorization, since the sequence would become static when it should evolve and be transformed into different versions. None the less, repetition of the sequence undoubtedly helps memorization to some extent. In the same way, when participants begin to read written texts, being able to re-read notes they have taken or been given does help the retention of linguistic material as in more traditional approaches.

So, although repetition continues to play its part, as in traditional approaches, we give more importance to the type of contact and the intensity of the relationship with the foreign language. We retain language when it engages us, when it produces an echo in us or responds to our needs and wishes for expression.

In LPD, there is never any pressure to retain everything since we consider that every participant has the right to choose. Participants are offered a wide choice of language into which they are free to dip and retain whatever they find relevant or useful.

2.5.1 Factors affecting retention

A number of factors contribute to the importance of retention in LPD:

- Participants are personally connected with and involved in their utterances, both affectively and intellectually. They are, therefore, more easily retained. The emotional and physical memory is as much engaged as the memory of the intellect.
- The language presented to the participants responds to their need for expression; being wanted, it is more readily accepted and assimilated.
- There is a high level of attentiveness which is characteristic of all group sessions.
- The atmosphere in the sessions encourages concentration and receptivity without tension or anxiety.
- Our approach to the use of language, encompassing movement, relaxation, bodily position, breathing, and auditory skills, stimulates the memory.

- There is no pressure to retain everything: everyone has the right to choose and to forget.
- The intensive character of LPD courses means that language items are presented frequently. The various types of language, including symbolic, poetic, and metaphoric, may be retained more readily.
- Practising the sounds of the language with movement encourages the rhythmic and phonic memory (Chapter 4).

2.6   The objectives of LPD

A central pedagogic objective in LPD is to continue to contribute to personal development generally as well as to the acquisition of language. Encouragement of those aptitudes, attitudes, and types of behaviour which will advance the two essential components of communication—receptiveness, and a capacity for expression—is fundamental to our approach. The exercises, in the context of an appropriate setting for learning, develop receptiveness, i.e. listening skills, openness, empathy, sensitivity towards oneself and others, intellectual development, observation skills, synthetic and analytical processes, and non-stressful concentration.

Such an approach involves two interlinked areas for developing a capacity for expression: the linguistic and the personal.

Linguistic

This includes a broadening of the capacity for rhythmic and melodic reproduction which assumes acquiring breathing and vocal techniques, a reinforcement of our capacity for synthesizing information in a new setting, of association, creativity, and a willingness to experiment. All this encourages our intellectual curiosity.

Personal

This includes a development of our spontaneity, creativity, willingness to become involved, of expressing ourselves as individuals, that is, the capacity not only to react but to respond personally to situations, taking risks and being prepared to make mistakes. It also helps to develop physical, emotional, and intellectual flexibility.

In LPD, the development of language skills contributes to the development of the whole individual while traditional teaching concentrates more exclusively on linguistic objectives and, above all, on the acquisition of structures and lexis. The empathetic atmosphere of the courses not only contributes to the development of the participants' self-confidence and motivates them to learn the language, but also develops their capacity to learn in general.

In traditional teaching, it has been observed that some learners have an extended vocabulary and cannot make use of it, others are excellent at grammar but have difficulty in speaking correctly or holding a conversation. Strictly linguistic criteria can be insufficient or inadequate in assessing language acquisition. In LPD, a pedagogy that focuses on the development of the individual in the context of linguistic performance, the acquisition of languages as a means of personal evolution stimulates linguistic performance. In other words, knowledge is retained more readily and powers of expression are increased.

2.7 Conclusion

In this chapter, we have tried to present a coherent methodological setting for psychodramaturgy. Some of the aspects we have discussed can contribute not only to psychodramaturgy but also to the communicative approach.

The common point is that both are oriented towards the participant (i.e. they put the participant in the centre of the acquisition process) and the way he or she relates to the foreign language. At the same time, they stress the two main functions of human language: the expressive and the communicative functions.

Psychodramaturgy does not only rely on a methodology which is different from the traditional one, but also on another practice. The coherence between theory and practice permits the latter to have the impact which we know it for. It is towards the concrete presentation of LPD that we are going to turn in the second part of the book.

PART TWO

Practical approaches to LPD

3 Relaxation

We start each day of an LPD course with a period of relaxation during which everyone taking part lies down on the floor. Relaxation techniques can just as easily be carried out by everyone sitting on chairs, which would be more applicable to usual classroom conditions. After presenting the reasons for using these techniques, I will explain how to lead classes in relaxation for people who are lying down, and people who are seated.

3.1 The effects and purposes of relaxation

Relaxation has an essential place in a teaching approach that takes into account the whole person, not only because of its relaxing effect but also because of the attitudes it encourages.

In the first place, relaxation can produce an immediate separation from the outside world, not only from whatever has happened before the class but also from one's general environment, so that it is possible to concentrate on the here and now. Relaxation techniques, done at the beginning of each day, provide a reassuring framework, a 'ritual' within which the group's activities can take place.

Relaxation allows participants a little private time for themselves; it helps them to become aware of their own selves before coming into contact with each other, or starting a group activity. While becoming aware of their bodies, they also tune in to their inner selves. They begin a process of interiorization before turning once again towards the world outside. There is a feeling of drawing closer to that deep, inner calm which lies latent within each of us, and of contact with its underlying energy. Relaxation leads us back to a state of creative openness which releases powers of imagination and expression. It stimulates receptivity at the sensorial level, and has a similar effect on ideas and emotions, which, in turn, has a positive effect on our capacity to memorize.

As well as developing self-confidence, relaxation provides a broader base for having confidence in others. By helping us to let go, to move on without fear of being lost, we are able to behave spontaneously, with a more positive attitude to whatever comes from within us or from outside. It encourages us to differentiate between ourselves and other people, to accept that we are individuals, with our own special characteristics. Comments made during a relaxation exercise such as 'That's my movement, that's my rhythm', take on a symbolic significance in the class and allow some participants to come to terms with the fact that they will make slower progress than others in some of the learning stages. Relaxation allows each of us to follow our own particular rhythm, to proceed at our own pace.

A continuous focus of attention on one's body during the exercises develops concentration: participants learn not to be distracted, to maintain contact with their body when thoughts may be disturbed by events going on around them.

Relaxation creates an atmosphere of calm and safety in the group which can give rise to confidence and openness. This increases the group's cohesion, and prepares the way for the release of creative spontaneity. Regarding language learning, relaxation offers unthreatening contact with the foreign language, instilling what might be called the primordial vocabulary of the body—words we need in order to define ourselves and to place ourselves in relation to time and space. For complete beginners, it also represents a first structuring of the language. The effects of relaxation exercises go beyond the classroom and are useful in generally motivating the day-to-day lives of participants; feeling involved in a learning process allows them to develop not just as members of the class but as individuals in their own right.

3.2   Relaxation in practice

3.2.1   The lying position

Presentation

Before starting the first relaxation class, some of the reasons for using it are given, and participants are asked if anyone has previous experience of relaxation techniques. It is explained that from the onset we will be adopting a holistic approach, which is to say, that we will not be aiming to relax one arm on one day, the other arm the next. This does happen in the early stages of some relaxation techniques. In LPD, we will bring about total relaxation of the whole body from the first session. Our procedures can differ in a number of ways from other techniques but, since the essence of what we are doing is to achieve a state of relaxation, participants used to relaxing in other ways are free to continue with them.

The sandwich method

To make sure that the participants have no problems in following the procedure, the instructions are given three times: first a sentence in the target language, then a translation in the first language so that they can follow the proceedings without struggling to understand, then once more in the target language, which is when we ask that they let the foreign language flow over them.

On the third day, we generally drop the translated phrase, though at the beginning of each new stage we do give participants a first-language equivalent of the key phrase. In most cases, instructions are given entirely in the target language from the fourth day, even for absolute beginners. By the fifth or sixth day, when we introduce the feeling of warmth, we translate only new elements. The ritualistic presentation of the instructions makes it easier for participants to remember the procedures and repeat them at home.

The position

Before starting the first relaxation class, we also present the reference position, that is the body position they can use and which they are free to vary according to their needs and what they find most comfortable. To do this, the animator lies down on his or her back, legs

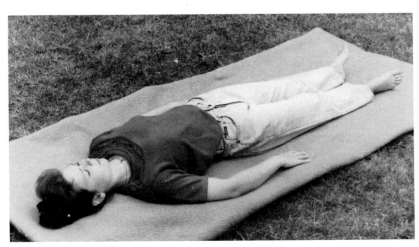

extended with feet slightly apart. The feet may be allowed to fall out-wards a little according to whatever feels most comfortable. The arms also lie a little away from the body, palms down and touching the floor. The participants are invited to close their eyes, since it helps concentration. If anyone prefers to keep their eyes open, they are naturally free to do so.

Procedure

When the participants are settled, the animator joins them, sitting on the floor, and lets a few seconds of silence pass by. This is to allow the participants time to relax but also for the animator's own benefit so that he or she can tune in to his or her body and state of mind before turning towards the group. The relaxation session then begins. A short pause is provided between the phrases in the target language, and between each sentence. In the text which follows, the first sentence is repeated in French as an example of the translation. The voice should be measured and low, but not too slow and deep, otherwise participants may fall asleep.

I am calm, (pause) relaxed, (pause) at peace.
Je suis calme, tranquille, paisible. (Translation)
I am calm, relaxed, at peace.

I feel my legs and my feet in contact with the floor.
(Translation)
My legs and feet are in contact with the floor.

I feel my pelvis in contact with the floor.
(Translation)
My pelvis is in contact with the floor.

I feel my back and my shoulders in contact with the floor.
(Translation)
My back and shoulders are in contact with the floor.

I feel my hands and my arms in contact with the floor.
(Translation)
My hands and arms are in contact with the floor.

I feel my head in contact with the floor.
(Translation)
My head is in contact with the floor.

My whole body is in contact with the floor.
(Translation)
I am calm, relaxed, at peace.
(Translation)

It will have been noted that we begin at the feet and gradually move upwards, as if our heads are observing our bodies from the bottom to the top. In the next stage, which concentrates on the weight of the body, we start with the right arm. This is because, at least in the case of right-handed people, it receives more conscious orders than any other part of the body, and is therefore the part of the body that has the closest conscious relationship with the brain. Again, there are pauses and each sentence is translated.

> Through the contact of my right hand and my right arm with the floor,
> (Translation)
> I feel the weight of my right hand and my right arm.
> (Translation)
> My right hand and arm are heavy, pleasantly heavy.
> (Translation)
>
> Through the contact of my left hand and my left arm with the floor,
> (Translation)
> I feel the weight of my left hand and my left arm.
> (Translation)
> My left hand and arm are heavy, pleasantly heavy.
> (Translation)
>
> Both my arms are heavy, pleasantly heavy.
> (Translation)
>
> Through the contact of my legs and my feet with the floor,
> (Translation)
> I feel the weight of my legs and my feet.
> (Translation)
> My legs and feet are heavy, pleasantly heavy.
> (Translation)
>
> Through the contact of my pelvis with the floor,
> (Translation)
> I feel the weight of my pelvis.
> (Translation)
> My pelvis is heavy, pleasantly heavy.
> (Translation)
>
> Through the contact of my back and my shoulders with the floor,
> (Translation)
> I feel the weight of my back and my shoulders.
> (Translation)

> My back and shoulders are heavy, pleasantly heavy.
> (Translation)
>
> Through the contact of my head with the floor,
> (Translation)
> I feel the weight of my head.
> (Translation)
> My head is heavy, pleasantly heavy.
> (Translation)
>
> My whole body is in contact with the floor,
> (Translation)
> My whole body is heavy, pleasantly heavy.
> (Translation)
> I am calm, relaxed, at peace.
> (Translation)

We allow the group a few moments to feel that sensation of contact and weight.

Then we draw their attention to the rhythm and movement of their breathing. Breathing is the most direct and most observable expression of our inner rhythm and of our changing emotions. In LPD, we use the breathing rhythm when trying to enter into empathetic contact with the protagonist during the double technique (Chapter 5). Breathing also determines the rhythm of the voice and this clearly has an important effect on how the individual expresses himself or herself.

Here are the phrases used to introduce the period when we concentrate on breathing:

> I feel the rhythm and the movement of my breathing.
> It is my rhythm, my breathing movement.
> I am calm, relaxed, at peace.

Then everyone can feel the rhythm and movement of their breathing for a while, perhaps as long as a minute. After a few days, when we begin to introduce the notion of warmth into the relaxation process, the following observations are made:

> Certain parts of my body are warmer than others. I feel that warmth and it spreads to every part of my body. Only my head stays cool, pleasantly cool, as if a light breeze were caressing my forehead.

Towards the fifth or sixth day of an intensive course we sometimes use a poem, one with a harmonious sound, such as, for French, Paul

Verlaine's *Le ciel est par-dessus le toit (The sky is above the roof)*.

We follow this by speaking in a firmer voice to introduce what we refer to as the 'Return phase' when the participants come back to awareness of the group and the room. Pauses and translation are used if necessary.

> Now come back, move your feet, tap the floor with your fingers. You can breathe deeply, feel the energy inside you. Before opening your eyes, imagine the room you are in. If you feel the need, stretch out. When you are ready, curl up slowly on your side, with a spiral movement, and sit up.

Finally, we invite feedback from the group, starting by asking participants if the rhythm was about right, too slow or too fast, and inviting their reactions to the animator's voice. This not only enables us to find out how well the rhythm suited the group but also encourages the group to start sharing their impressions. This feedback is especially important in the first few days since it gives the animator an opportunity to adjust to the group and to discuss any reactions from participants.

3.2.2   The seated position

> Participants are asked to make themselves comfortable in their chairs, legs extending naturally from the pelvis, hands on thighs, and preferably with their backs touching the back of the chair.
>
> The principles are the same as for relaxation in a lying position. We begin with a contact stage, then we introduce the group to the feeling of weight. Here is one sequence that can be used in this relaxation exercise:

> I am calm, (pause) relaxed, (pause) at peace.
> Je suis calme, tranquille, paisible. (Translation)
> I am calm, relaxed, at peace.

> I feel the contact of my feet with the floor.
> (Translation)
> My feet are in contact with the floor.

> I feel my legs and pelvis in contact with the chair.
> (Translation)
> My legs and my pelvis are in contact with the chair.

> I feel my back in contact with the chair.
> (Translation)
> My back is in contact with the chair.

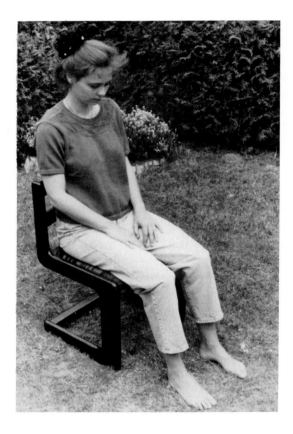

I feel my hands and arms in contact with my legs.
(Translation)
My hands and arms are in contact with my legs.

I feel my head in contact with my neck.
(Translation)
My head is in contact with my neck.

My whole body is in contact with the floor and with the chair.
(Translation)
I am calm, relaxed, at peace.

The next stage concerning the weight of the body is also similar to the lying position.

Through the contact of my right hand and my right arm with my right leg,
(Translation)
I feel the weight of my right hand and my right arm.
(Translation)

My right hand and arm are heavy, pleasantly heavy.
(Translation)

Through the contact of my left hand and my left arm with my left leg,
(Translation)
I feel the weight of my left hand and my left arm.
(Translation)
My left hand and arm are heavy, pleasantly heavy.
(Translation)

Both my arms are heavy, pleasantly heavy.
(Translation)

Through the contact of my feet with the floor,
(Translation)
I feel the weight of my feet and my legs.
(Translation)
My feet and legs are heavy, pleasantly heavy.
(Translation)

Through the contact of my legs and pelvis with the chair,
(Translation)
I feel the weight of my legs and my pelvis.
(Translation)
My legs and my pelvis are heavy, pleasantly heavy.
(Translation)

Through the contact of my back and shoulders with the chair,
(Translation)
I feel the weight of my back and shoulders.
(Translation)
My back and shoulders are heavy, pleasantly heavy.
(Translation)

Through the contact of my head with my neck,
(Translation)
I feel the weight of my head.
(Translation)
My head is heavy, pleasantly heavy.
(Translation)

My whole body is heavy, pleasantly heavy.
(Translation)
I am calm, relaxed, at peace.
(Translation)

As in the description for the lying position, this is followed by concentration on the rhythm and movement of their breathing, after which we continue with the 'Return stage'.

3.2.3 Possible side-effects

There are a number of possible reactions which might take participants by surprise, and for which the animator has to be prepared. These cases are rare, but it is as well to know what to do should they arise.

Hyperventilation

This is the most visible of the possible physical side-effects. It tends to affect those who are so anxious to perform well that they breathe too deeply when the body is resting; an excess of oxygen leads to a mild form of hyperventilation. This is marked by pins and needles in the hands or legs and can be relieved by pressing the hands together repeatedly while at the same time pressing down with the feet. This physical effort re-establishes the balance. Participants should be advised to let their breathing come and go in its natural rhythm, without trying to breath more deeply than the body requires.

Muscular pain

In rare cases, participants feel a slight muscular pain after the relaxation exercise. This pain is the result of relaxing a part of the body that we previously stretched. It is what we all feel after we have kept a muscle stretched for a period of time, an outstretched arm, for instance, and then changed its position. In fact, it is a positive reaction. Participants who do too much and put themselves under stress, may experience a slight tiredness. It is only a little later that they will feel the regenerative effects of relaxation.

Feeling cold

This is sometimes experienced when warmth is introduced into the class routine for the first time since it heightens some participants' awareness of cold and they notice the contrast. This phenomenon disappears within a few days.

Palpitations

In general, this sensation is only found in relaxation classes where people have been encouraged to concentrate on their heart rhythm—something to avoid. Any person who experiences this feeling should be encouraged to imagine something that will reassure them, for instance, the rhythm of a horse slowly climbing a gentle slope or rain dripping from the petal of a flower, and that their heart is beating calmly to the same rhythm.

Loss of concentration

While the above phenomena are extremely unusual, lack of concentration is very common, even though relaxation provides a very good training in concentration. It is not a matter of fighting extraneous thoughts that only creates tension, but of letting them float by like clouds in the sky. I recall with pleasure the metaphor which compares thoughts to guests in one's home; they are passing through and should not take possession.

3.2.4   Other techniques

Here are more techniques to induce a period of relaxation or concentration.

The open hand

1 We owe this technique to Ilse Middendorf from Berlin whose work involves the inter-relation of respiratory and bodily movement (Middendorf 1984).

Concentrate on your closed right hand. As you breath in, open your hand slowly, so that breathing and body movement coincide. As you breathe out, close your hand. Repeat the same exercise three times. Then, after a pause, repeat the same sequence with the left hand. This quick and easy technique develops inward concentration, and it has a relaxing effect.[1]

The rainbow

Close your eyes and imagine that you are looking at the colours of the rainbow, one after the other—red, orange, yellow, green, blue, indigo, violet—then, after a moment, open your eyes. You may wish to add to this technique by imagining the colours again but in reverse order, with the eyes still closed. This often has an energizing effect, though the effect varies from one person to another, and each participant will come to find a particular colour they prefer to have in mind at the end of this exercise.

The clenched fist

2 This technique is based on a principle of Jacobsonian relaxation, namely that of alternating tension and relaxation (Jacobson 1929, 1962).

Stretch out your right arm, close the fist, and squeeze tightly. Then relax and let the arm drop to your side. Feel the difference between your right and left arm. Do the same with your left arm, then with your right leg, left leg, both legs, and your pelvis.[2]

Numbers

Close your eyes and imagine that just above the horizon you can see the number five, then four, then three, two, and finally one. Each number is accompanied by a deep outward breath during which you feel that you are becoming more and more relaxed. Stay relaxed for a moment, then count back from one to five. As you come to three, imagine that by the time you reach five you will be relaxed, and full of energy.[3]

It is possible to associate meanings with the numbers, for example:

5   I am here, present.
4   I am aware of my body.
3   I am aware of my breathing.
2   I am calm, relaxed, at peace.
1   I am more and more deeply calm ...

Integration

You could use this technique at the end of each session.

The participants take up a relaxed position, become aware of their contact with the floor, concentrate on the rhythm and movement of their breathing, and open their thoughts to whichever words and sentences in the target language happen to come to mind.

This approach of 'letting words and sentences come of their own accord' seems to help participants to assimilate the new language more easily. It represents a useful transitional stage before coming back to the world outside.

You could use the same approach every time you close a book and prepare yourself for the next activity. This allows you to let your memory recollect what you have read but at the same time to consider what you have read with another perspective. You can experience associated thoughts which may come to mind, and disengage yourself from one activity before becoming involved in the next.

3.3   Conclusion

It is worth noting that the above relaxation technique has been derived from observation of people in a relaxed state. It has been noted that people in that state have a sensation of heaviness and of warmth, so it is by inducing heaviness and warmth that we bring about a state of relaxation. It is an inverted process: we work backwards from the symptoms to reach the relaxed state.

[3] This technique is derived from Silva Mind Control (Silva 1977).

The relaxation technique described derives from a combination of the physical and environmental, as well as intellectual, impact on therapeutic techniques applied to the body.[4]

In contrast with relaxation techniques which are based on auto-suggestion, the technique we adopt is based on a logical principle: through contact we can have an immediate sense of weight, and therefore of heaviness. No doubt this explains why our participants are able to feel this sensation very quickly, whereas, with techniques based on auto-suggestion it takes several days.

The process of relaxation in LPD has two stages. The first is one of discovery: 'I am becoming aware of being in contact with ...', 'I am aware of the weight of ...'. The second is one of acceptance of a particular physical state: 'My feet are in contact ...', or 'My feet are heavy ...'. It is undeniable that this two-stage induction, one of active perception, the other of awareness and acceptance, gives a structure to the inner development of the relaxation exercise. At the same time, it develops an attitude which is important in life: every conscious change we make is based on perceiving and accepting reality (instead of using up energy to deny reality, however unpalatable it may be to us). Our relaxation process is in keeping with the spirit of individualism which characterizes our pedagogic approach. For example, when warmth has been induced, each participant's experience of that warmth is entirely personal, and is not in accordance with any pre-arranged plan.

After several days, the relaxation process has become very familiar and we change from using 'I' to 'you' in our instructions: 'You are becoming aware ...', we ask the participants to make the transfer into the first person. In this way, they are able to change the exercise into something of their own. This may also create a productive distance between them and us.

On the last day or two of an intensive two-week course, the relaxation exercises take place without any spoken accompaniment. The animator lies down on the floor with the group but participants perform the exercises by themselves, at their own pace, and so are prepared for continuing on their own once the course is over.

I think it is important to take one's time with these exercises. Some animators worry that participants will become bored by this sort of exercise. That is not at all the case provided one does not take it too far. It is necessary to compare one's own rhythm with the group's in the feedback session to make sure that the relaxation session does not have an opposite effect to what is intended.

I would not consider it appropriate to recommend any strenuous activity immediately after relaxation. I sometimes give the group a vocal exercise involving a poem with gentle rhythms, or perhaps an activity that requires only slow movements.

When I train teachers in relaxation techniques I ask them not to lead a relaxation session until they have practised the exercises themselves every day for three weeks. We can only really communicate what we have experienced.

4 Rhythm and expression

1 An earlier version of this chapter was originally published in *Le Français dans le Monde* (1986 no. 205). We are grateful to the publishers for allowing us to use it in this book.

This chapter begins with a description of the part played by intonation in language learning and communication.[1] It then presents exercises for developing an awareness of rhythm and melody in the foreign language. The exercises using total body movement help develop a corresponding 'whole body' feeling for the musical aspects of the language.

4.1 The role of intonation in foreign language learning

The best music is the sound of the voice. [KESSEL]

In LPD, the approach to the foreign language begins by concentrating on its rhythms, tones, and melody. Participants are made aware of these elements and are encouraged to reproduce them. Several intermediate exercises for reinforcing that sense of rhythm and melody are included below.

Intonation and expression

A capacity for self-expression is central to all language acquisition. In our view, learners should be the authors of their own speech: everyone has something to communicate, real or imaginary, directed to others or inwardly to themselves. In LPD, the message is inseparable from the people who give it sense and value. The function of intonation is to help a person's spoken words to resonate and live, and to express all the elements of the message, that is to say, its emotional and personal as well as its intellectual components.

Learners begin to imprint their own personalities on language from the moment they are able to express their needs, desires, sensations, and feelings. This imprint is conveyed especially by intonation; words communicate experience, and intonation indicates the meaning and importance of that experience. Speech informs us of speakers' intentions, of their involvement, how much commitment they feel, their relationship with the listener, and the atmosphere in which the communication takes place. Speech conveys meaning as well as sense. To take a simple example, if I know how to say 'She is pleasant' but not 'She is unpleasant' I can still make my meaning clear by changing my tone of voice. Language is brought to life in intonation and expression.

Intonation and comprehension

The decoding of language undergoes a process of transformation which has as much to do with the emotions as with the intellect. Special attention is paid to tone of voice, variation in rhythm, and modulation of intonation. The emotional overtones of what is expressed can have a decisive effect on the meaning of the message; it is important to sensitize learners to these aspects. In LPD, participants become more alert to what the speaker is trying to communicate, and to the balance between what is said and what is expressed, how things are said, and what is really meant. Intonation conveys the signals necessary for true understanding and has the same importance in the classroom that we give to it, however unconsciously, in everyday life.

Intonation and retention

Memory is stimulated when rhythm and melody are taken into account. The language practised in our exercises is full of such characteristics and, being personal, it is much easier to assimilate. Accompanying the poetic elements with movement etches the text in the body and mind so that it is progressively assimilated without being consciously learnt by heart.

4.2   A practical approach to intonation

Most of the exercises described in this section can be used with complete beginners. In this way, they are introduced early to the rhythms and forms of expression in the foreign language. The exercises develop their sensitivity to sound, so that their speech begins to express more of an inner feeling for the foreign language. The exercises can also put the group in a good relaxed mood which helps with group bonding.

The first exercises offer a variety of approaches to rhythm. Some can be used with any language, while others, which may be specific to French, can be adapted to other languages. Other exercises follow which encourage *expression* in the foreign language, an ability to sense what lies behind words, what it is that a speaker wants to convey.

4.2.1 Rhythm

To encounter a foreign language is at first like experiencing a new rhythm. The rhythm provides a structural framework into which melodies and sounds can fit. So, in LPD, we begin by making sure that participants are sensitive to the importance of rhythm in communication. First, we help them to recognize what is specific about their *own* rhythm. Then we begin exercises based on natural rhythms found in the foreign language.

Listening to the breathing pattern

We are indebted to Ilse Middendorf in Berlin, and in particular one of her students, H. von Hochberg, for the basis of these exercises.

We encourage participants to become aware of their own breathing pattern on which the speech pattern will be superimposed. We also use exercises which combine breathing patterns and body movement, in which the individual is able to increase his or her breathing without changing its natural pattern.[2]

The breathing duet

The participants form pairs. They begin by concentrating on their individual breathing, observing how it comes quite naturally, and without trying to control or change it in any way. Next, they try to breathe to the same rhythm as their partners, adopting the same position, observing whatever new feelings and impressions arise. Then they resume their own patterns.

This exercise leads them towards a greater awareness of the other person, teaches them to tune themselves into another person and to adopt an unfamiliar breathing pattern—something they will have to get used to in the foreign language too.

Echo-rhythms

The class forms a circle. Each member taps out a rhythm in turn on a tambourine or by clapping their hands; the sound is reproduced in echo by the class as a whole. When the atmosphere is appropriately united, we suggest that individuals use a rhythm to express whatever feeling or impression comes to mind—a skipping rhythm, for example, to express happiness.

This short exercise introduces simple rhythmic variations which the learners will also have to do in the foreign language. We often follow on from this exercise by asking participants to create a rhythm that reflects the foreign language, for example, stressing the last beat in French.

In step with your partner

The participants move around the room listening to their own rhythm and to the other individuals, who are creating rhythms with their feet as they walk. We ask them to join another person who is using a rhythm similar to their own and then to join in. When two partners are walking to the same rhythm, they start to introduce variations (as one does in a conversation) before reverting to their earlier shared rhythm. This exercise encourages a 'whole body' awareness of the other person's rhythm, and an ability to adopt that rhythm without losing one's own sense of self.

Speaking tambourines

The class forms a circle. The animator, with one tambourine, passes another to someone on the other side of the circle, and initiates a brief 'dialogue', using the tambourines and mime; the tambourines are then passed to others who continue the exercise. This sort of exercise shows that it is possible to use rhythm and mime to express meaning and establish a relationship, that words are not indispensable. In showing just how rhythmic variations can communicate meaning, it introduces participants to a new way of listening.

The conductors

Two groups face each other. Each appoints a 'conductor' who has to beat out a rhythm on a tambourine (or clap). This rhythm is taken up by members of each group, who clap in time. The two groups begin to walk around the room, following their respective leaders, who vary the intensity of the rhythms as the mood takes them. The two groups change their clapping repeatedly to keep time with the conductors, which creates a sort of rhythmic dialogue. In one variation, group A's conductor stands in the middle of group B, and vice versa. The conductors have to keep up their chosen rhythm even though they may be surrounded by people making a different sound. This is like sticking to one's own opinion when surrounded by people who have a different point of view.

West Side

Two groups, A and B, face each other from opposite ends of the room. The leader of group A, standing one pace in front, beats a rhythm on a tambourine (or claps); the rest of the A group claps their hands in time. When the rhythm has been firmly established, the leader, followed by the whole of group A, walks towards group B; when the two leaders meet, group A gradually fades out its rhythm, while leader B starts up a new rhythm. As soon as everyone in group B can keep time with their hands, their conductor leads them towards the opposite end of the room. Group A withdraws silently. When they arrive at the end of the room, the group A leader passes the tambourine (if there is one) to someone else, who starts a new rhythm.[3]

3 We owe this exercise to Augusto Boal (Boal 1983: 105).

The rumour

Two groups, A and B, line up facing each other, one metre apart. A participant at one end of line A beats a rhythm which is taken up by the rest of line A. When the rhythm has been established, the participant walks between the two lines; the sound is taken up by each member of line B as the participant walks past them so that, when he or she reaches the end of the line, the whole class is playing the same rhythm. A participant from line B then claps out a new rhythm, and so on, until everyone has had a turn. As well as being an interesting exercise in rhythm, this also works well in developing the group's cohesion and attention to sounds.

4 and 1

The class sits in a circle. Participant A beats once on the floor with the left hand, then with the right hand, then left, and right. On the fourth beat, his or her neighbour, B, makes the first beat with the left hand. So A's right hand and B's left hand rise and fall together. B completes the second, third, and fourth beats, at which point C joins in with the first beat, and so on. This exercise is derived from traditional rhythm games.

When the rhythm has been repeated once or twice, participants can be asked to continue with a phrase using the same rhythm and number of beats which can be repeated in turn until another participant suggests a new phrase.

Crossed hands

The class forms a circle, sitting on the floor in the middle of the room with their hands by their sides. Participant A puts both hands on the floor. B hooks his or her left arm under A's right arm, then puts both hands on the floor. C does the same, and so on. At the other end of the circle, the last participant, X, is to the left of A. Participant A beats the ground with the left hand, X does the same with the right, followed by B with the left, A with the right, and so on. Different rhythms can be introduced, for instance, by beating once with the left hand and twice with the right. When the exercise has been thoroughly practised, we sometimes ask participants to beat in time with a poem which has a strong rhythm, such as a nursery rhyme or a verse from an early pop song.[4] For example, in French *La môme néant* by Jean Tardieu and *Le pélican* by Robert Desnos. In English, *Jazz Chants* by Caroline Grahams.

All the above exercises train participants to listen to and play with rhythm. They also help concentration and often have the effect of reinforcing class cohesion.

[4] We owe this exercise to Anthony Clark, a teacher of English in Poland.

4.2.2   Exercises in French rhythms

This section looks at exercises devised with the rhythm of French in mind. Readers may like to adapt the examples to the languages they are teaching. For English, the main beat will often be the first, as in 'Hickory, Dickory, **Dock**'.

Number in rhythm

This type of exercise, taken from Laura Sheleen, has been adapted to French rhythm (in the English original the first beat of each measure was tonic).

Rhythm in triple time

Participants strike twelve times with their hands a series of measures with three beats in each, stressing the last beat of each measure (i.e. putting the tonic accent on the last syllable of each rhythmic group). So we have: 1 2 **3** / 4 5 **6** / 7 8 **9** / 10 11 **12**.

Rhythm in four time

This is also in twelve beats, but this time as a series of measures with four beats in each, with stress on the fourth beat:
1 2 3 **4** / 5 6 7 **8** / 9 10 11 **12**.

Simultaneous rhythms

The class divides into two. Group A strikes the three-time beat and group B strikes the four-time beat, then vice versa.

Alternating rhythms

Group A strikes in three-time for twelve beats then in four-time for twelve beats; group B the reverse. In some classes it may be possible to carry this out as a walking exercise, with the feet stamping on the floor on the tonic. In order for these rhythms not to remain an abstraction but to be experienced in relation to French, at a later stage we ask the class to replace the beats with words, e.g. 'liberté' in three-time, 'égalité' in four-time, and texts made up of short sentences, e.g. 'je le **pense**/ je le **crois**/ je le **veux**/ je le **peux**' (= 1 2 **3**/ 4 5 **6**/ 7 8 **9**/ 10 11 **12**).

Dialogues can be created in 12 beats, as follows:

Group A	C'est a **nous**? (question)	1	2	**3**
Group B	C'est a **vous**! (confirmation)	4	5	**6**
Group A	C'est bien **vrai**?	7	8	**9**
Group B	Mais bien **sûr**.	10	11	**12**

Participants may like to make up rhymes in three- and four-time rhythm,—even sonnets in which the first two stanzas are in three-time and the last two in four-time.

Three-time examples	*Four-time examples*
Je suis **là**	Regarde-**moi**,
Devant **toi**	Écoute-**moi**,
C'est bien **moi**.	Car, je suis **là**.
Toujours **moi**	

Following the same principle, we sometimes suggest writing a poem using only imperatives, for example:

Viens chez **moi**
Dépèche-**toi**
Assieds-**toi**
Écoute-**moi**

We have also used the same sort of exercise with past participles and later suggested Jean Tardieu's poem *Participes* (*Participles*), which is made up of a series of participles.

Discovering a poem by a well-known writer that has been made up using only participles can have a strong motivating effect on the creative feeling of some students.

Progressive rhythm

The class beats time with the following rhythm:

1/1 2/1 2 3/1 2 3 4/1 2 3/1 2/1

A march can be set to these rhythms: one step forward on the first beat, two steps back on the second, and so on, emphasizing the tonic with the heel. Words can be set to the same rhythms, for example:

Oui, c'est **vrai**, il l'a **fait**, il me l'a **dit**.

1 /   1   2 / 1   2   3 / 1 2   3 **4**

Victor Hugo's poem below is constructed according to the same principle. Here are the first three stanzas by way of illustration:

Les Djinns

Murs, ville	Dans la plaine	La voix plus haute
Et port,	Naît un bruit.	Semble un grelot,
Asile	C'est l'haleine	D'un nain qui saute
de Mort,	De la nuit.	C'est le galop.
Mer grise	Elle brame	Il fuit, s'élance.
Où brise	Comme une âme	Puis en cadence
La brise	Qu'une flamme	Sur un pied danse
Tout dort.	Toujours suit.	Au bord d'un flot.

We have also created exercises in which the class, in a circle, pass batons in time with a sentence or a poem (Dufeu 1986).

Rhythms and poems

Poems express the rhythmic characteristics of a language very clearly. Some can be accompanied by rhythmic movements without losing their appeal. Here are examples for particular characteristics which fit the rhythm of French.

We use *Le pélican* by Robert Desnos in particular, first clapping and then walking to its rhythm, the feet picking out the rhythm and the arms moving in time to the melody (Dufeu 1986). Jean Tardieu's poem, *La môme néant*, with its abundance of plosives ('Quoi qu'a dit ...') reinforces that impression of metronomic rhythm which is a hallmark of the French language. *Les Djinns* by Hugo (see above), in which each new line is extended by one beat, gives a very strong sense of rhythm and of tonic emphasis. *Pâques* by Paul Claudel is composed of a series of monosyllables repeated three times over, which reinforces the impression of rhythmic regularity. This poem, with a similar structure, also lends itself to very effective choral work.

Colours

Blue, blue, blue,
Blue are your eyes.

> Black, black, black,
> Black is your hair.

> White, white, white,
> White is your skin.

> Red, red, red,
> Red is your blood.

> Green, green, green,
> Green is your hope.

It is possible to identify poems written in any target language, which have similar characteristics, especially in metre, onomatopoeia, repetition, alliteration, assonance, and rhyme.

4.3 An approach to expression

The sound is haunted by the meaning. [VALÉRY]

4.3.1 Vocal expression

Learners often tend to speak rather lifelessly in the foreign language, which reflects the fact that it has been taught to them throughout their school lives with its emotional content removed. They need help to rediscover the expressiveness of the sounds in that language, not simply to transcribe unfamiliar sounds. In LPD, we do this by sensitizing them to vocal nuances. In this way, they begin to feel the impact of sound on meaning, that it is sound which conveys meaning.

Sensitizing the body to sound

We try to make participants aware of our body's zones of sound resonance, the effects of their vibration, and their influence on breathing movement (Middendorf 1984: 60). For example, we ask them to pronounce a /u:/ while noticing that this sound has a special zone of resonance in the pelvis, or /ɔ: / at the position of the sternum, etc. This exercise not only makes us more perceptive of nuances in sounds, but also develops our awareness of breathing patterns. It is yet another way to encourage concentration.

Voices in echo

The class forms pairs. Participant A suggests a series of sounds or says a phrase in a given tone. Participant B tries to repeat the phrase as exactly as possible. A repeats the phrase until he or she feels that B's voice is making an exact echo, after which they reverse roles. This exercise leads to the decoding of the nuances of what A intended to express and enables A to hear what was said from a fresh perspective.

Later, the pairs may like to try another exercise in which each pair starts by exchanging a series of sounds. They separate. The As close their eyes and must find the other member of the pair, B, who is repeating the sound series A had produced. We might ask participants to make up a short sequence around the sound /u:/ for instance, so they would be trying to find their partners in a forest of /u:/ sounds.

The expressive word
Participants walk around the room, repeating in a low voice any word they are particularly fond of, or consider very expressive (in French, for instance, 'murmure'). They then say the word out loud to everyone they meet, trying to give expression to what they find so special about the word. The sound becomes the conveyor of meaning.

Interrogations
The class walks round the room, pronouncing the interrogative pronouns What? How? Why? trying out a variety of intonations. The exercise may be continued with dialogues.

H'm!
Participants walk around the room saying 'H'm!' in different tones. The same exercise can be carried out with other interjections.

Mirror in series
Though based on the same principle as the previous exercise, in this exercise participants divide into groups and go to different parts of the room. One after another these groups echo the animator's words and gestures.

Polarities
The class form pairs and take turns to stage a short play in which participant A says 'Yes' and B answers 'No'. For example, A invites B to dance, and B refuses by saying 'No'.

These short scenes serve to demonstrate how far the meaning of simple words can vary according to context, situation, and the individuals concerned. They also increase everyone's awareness of the connotative values of the statements, and serve to integrate body language and vocal expression. They can also lead on to role-playing, in which the actors develop the same theme using their own words.

One way of preparing participants for this exercise is to ask them to walk around the room saying 'Yes' or 'No' to each person they meet before joining up in pairs. By this time, they may already have some feeling for the many nuances of expression in the varieties of 'Yes' and 'No' they have heard.

Polysemic phrases
The class divides into groups of two or three to present a short performance in which they will use a precise polysemic phrase, such as 'It's over', or 'That's enough', or 'I can't'. Interjections such as 'How?' can also be used. Different meanings arise according to the situation, the people represented in the 'play', and the meaning given to the phrase.

4.3.2   Speech and body language

Of course, our bodies participate directly in the expression of a message indicating the difference between the literal meaning of the words used and what is actually being expressed. The body supports the message, modulates its meaning, reinforces or contradicts the verbal statement. The body can also make sense out of silence. Observing the body helps us to identify the underlying meaning of the unspoken as we listen.

'Embodied' words
Participants form pairs and practise representing a noun, such as solitude, liberty, curiosity, suspicion, tenderness, warmth, or an adverb. A uses body language to show the word; B says the word, suggesting the way A expresses it and what sensation or impression it produces. Afterwards, the same technique can be used to give spoken and physical expression to opposites, yes/no, always/never, night/day, etc.: A adopts a manner which suggests 'yes' and says the word. B adopts a stance that indicates the opposite, and says 'no'. An alternative would be to have the whole class try to find out the word represented by the actor before saying it out loud. This 'play' with words reinforces the contribution of body language to verbal expression as well as of tone of voice to meaning.

Body, vocal, and verbal doubling
This exercise comes from the body-work tradition of psychodrama. We have added a vocal phase to it.

A adopts a position. B takes up the same position behind A, as double, at the same time translating in sounds or interjections what A's position suggests. C then expresses his or her own impression of A's pose, taking up a position as double on B's other side. For example, A expresses tiredness, B translates it with a slow, heavy 'Ah'; C says 'I can't go on', 'I'm tired'. A maintains his or her position so that other participants can take over from B and C and act out their own interpretation of A's position.

Double bodily dialogue
Participant A adopts a position which suggests a feeling or thought. Participant B completes the tableau by representing a complementary position. Other participants take turns to double with A and B. This technique can lead into a dialogue, with A and B re-perfoming what they feel was most relevant in the exercise, and engaging in a conversation during which others continue to act as their doubles.[5]

5 We owe this technique to Daniel Feldhendler.

Speech, silence, speech
A short scene or sequence is acted out by two participants. On a signal from the animator the participants stop speaking, using only mime and gestures to continue the dialogue. On a second signal from the animator, the participants continue the performance with words. This develops their vocal expressiveness in the new spoken phase. Students tend to respond very enthusiastically to this exercise.[6]

6 This technique has been taken from Augusto Boal.

Poetry and movement

Poems bring out the rhythmic and melodic characteristics of the foreign language. They are rich in expression and connotations. When poetry is combined with movement it becomes easier to remember—perhaps because it is experienced and absorbed by the whole body. As Jousse (1974) has shown, our use of movement is like the rhythmic swaying of children when they recite poetry, or of those groups with a strong oral tradition when they recite texts such as the Koran or Old Testament.

The following section illustrates four ways in which movement can be used as an accompaniment to poetry.

Space and Time

The Past is behind me
The Future is in front of me
But the Present is in me.

This poem is said to a sideways swaying of the whole body, with the legs apart for stability. The movement stems from the pelvis; starting from beside the left hip, the hands are raised above and to the right of the right shoulder.

The first three lines are spoken in a gradually rising melodic 'curve' (described by Delattre (1965) as a 'continuation curve') while the arms are moved upwards and across, from left to right; the arms are brought back to their original position between each line, in silence. The last line is spoken in a falling curve—which Delattre calls a 'finality curve'—while the arms are slowly lowered to their original position.

As soon as the participants are familiar with the words and movements they are asked to repeat the text, but now imagining that they are making the movements, not actually doing so.

There are so many English poems which can be recited with movement. An excellent selection is available in *Speak Out! 'Rhymes and Rhythm'* (Vaughan-Rees 1991).

Instead of asking participants to accompany a poem with a movement of the whole body, we sometimes suggest that they try saying it while making a micro-movement—lifting and lowering the index finger, for example, in time with rising and falling cadences. This alternative approach is particularly helpful to those with motor difficulties.

Semantic gesture

This is a technique in which the gesture ends on the tonic syllable. Here is a poem which lends itself to this approach:

Listen to me

You see my eyes
But you don't see me.
You hear my voice
But you don't hear me.
Listen to your heart
You'll understand me.
(An adaptation of a poem by Yann Marzin from 'Radioscopie' on 30 April 1981)

On 'You see my eyes', participants make a hand movement which ends on 'my eyes', with the index finger touching the bone beneath the eye. On 'But you don't see me' the hands curl slightly to cover the eyes, and so on with the other lines. Groups can be formed afterwards to work out alternative hand movements.

There are many poems in English which can be recited with hand movement. An obvious choice is Stevie Smith's poem below with the speaker plucking petals from an imagined flower:

Tender Only to One

Tender only to one
Tender and true
The petals swing
To my fingering
Is it you, or you, or you?

Sound correction through poetry

We cannot emphasize too much how important it is for learners to have a good understanding of key sound differences. Native speakers tend to cope with such differences by subconsciously referring to context, but the foreign learner, who is unable to distinguish between voiceless and voiced sounds (in French he or she will assume that 'ils sont'/'ils ont', 'vous savez'/'vous avez', etc. are homophones) has significant decoding problems. Some southern Germans, in particular, have trouble distinguishing between voiceless fricatives /f/, /s/, /ʃ/, and voiced fricatives /v/, /z/, /ʒ/. Their learning habits in their own dialect create an auditory block which prevents them from recognizing what, in French, are important characteristics.

We make up poems which help participants to become aware of these phonological opposites, again using body rhythm. The following is an example of a phonetic poem written with these particular problems in mind:

Sons et Zons

De la précision
De la décision
De la concision

Nous y songeons
Quand nous changeons
Les sons ets les zons

When the poem is spoken, the left hand is raised to mark a voiceless consonant such as /p/, /t/, /k/, /f/, /s/, /ʃ/ and then lowered sharply.

The right hand is moved slowly forwards, palm out, as if resisting an air current, to mark a voiced consonant such as /z/.

Mobile poem
In this activity, each participant is responsible for a particular line or series of lines from a poem. They walk round the room, taking up a different position relative to each other, and the poem changes each time the series of lines are repeated. Participants are encouraged to vary the melodic curve of their lines to reflect this new context and any new meaning which the change suggests. The exercise is repeated several times, each new grouping leading to a new pattern of rising and falling intonations. *Déjeuner du matin* by Jacques Prévert and *Monsieur* by Marc Argaud (Moget and Neveu 1975: 95) work well in this exercise.

Sometimes we ask participants to indicate by their position how long they would like to pause between what they say and what was said before. This gives us a spatial description of the poem's rhythm.

We have carried out a choral exercise which uses the same spatial presentation technique using poems such as Apollinaire's *Mutations* and Paulin's *L'oiseau sauvage*.

4.4 Conclusion

In teaching, the more we do to help learners express themselves, the more the language reflects their real and imaginary lives, and the greater the significance of the messages they can exchange between each other. This explains, among other things, the important place that must be given to intonation in the learning process.

5 Linguistic psychodramaturgy in practice

This chapter describes the main stages of a course in linguistic psychodramaturgy (LPD), as well as some of its underlying principles. It includes a number of practical exercises which readers will be able to adapt to their particular classroom needs.

5.1 The teaching environment

5.1.1 The space

Classes take place in a carpeted room without tables or chairs and participants sit or lie on the floor. Since there is no furniture, everyone is free to take up the space as they choose, to decide where they want to be in relation to others, and to the group as a whole. The fact that the space can be used in a variety of ways is important because it means that everyone is able to move very freely, both individually and as a group. One effect is to intensify self-awareness and concentration.

Having an open space to work in obviously helps with several exercises: the double technique (p. 94) is easier, for instance, when participants are not sitting at desks. The same applies to the warm-up exercises (p. 93). And this unfamiliar classroom gives participants the chance to behave in a new, less constrained way; the new setting thus encourages new attitudes towards the unfamiliar foreign language. It also makes it easier to overcome traditional notions about teaching and those past learning experiences which possibly bring back unhappy memories. So, a different workspace encourages a fresh outlook.

5.1.2 The timetable

LPD works best when used intensively, i.e. between three and six classroom hours per day whether over weekends (fifteen hours) or one or two weeks (thirty hours per week). It could be argued that this highly intensive approach, together with our methods of working and the concentration by animators on the participants' wish to express themselves, combine to give learners an even closer relationship with the target language than if they were living in the country where it is spoken.

5.1.3   The participants

So far, we have worked with adults between twenty and seventy-one years of age, the majority of whom were aged between thirty and forty-five. Their educational background was mixed, ranging from those who had never experienced secondary school to others with university degrees.

We have experimented with only one course for adolescents aged fourteen. The main difference identified in this experience was that we had to use more intermediate exercises with them. The result was considered to be a success—but not only in terms of language acquisition; we noticed a clear change in their attitudes to learning, with marked improvements in their attention span and powers of concentration. In the feedback sessions, many of these adolescents told us they had been surprised to discover that what other participants said in a foreign language could be interesting and this had encouraged them to pay more attention to what others had to say. In the same way, trainers who are now using LPD techniques in schools report improvements in class participation and motivation as well as in performance.

We work with groups from various cultural backgrounds and have found that this encourages learners to help each other.

5.1.4   Entry levels in relation to the curriculum

We have two levels or stages for entry to our courses (Figure 8, at the end of this chapter). We do not aim for homogeneity in classes nor for a standard learning process, though teaching a mixed group of complete beginners clearly requires considerable experience and sensitivity.

Stage one, corresponding to the first two weeks of study, is intended for beginners and false beginners, and provides an initiation into the target language. However, we have also had advanced learners on this course who have used it to deepen and extend their existing knowledge.

Stage two is used for advanced learners. It begins in the third week of the course (Figure 8). Because of the approach we follow, even non-native teachers of the target language have found these classes very worthwhile.

The curriculum and the participant's progress from one stage to the next follow a spiral pattern. It would be difficult for complete beginners to move on to our second stage after only two weeks' introductory classes, so we advise them to repeat that section again. Since the content of the courses changes all the time and the exercises vary with each new group, those repeating the course are able to improve their knowledge from a different starting point and so become better prepared for the second stage. After a two-week course, we recommend that learners take a break of at least seven days, during which time their minds can continue to piece together and give shape to what they have learnt.

5.1.5 Size of class

The ideal size for a class, especially during the first three learning steps (5.2.1, 5.2.2, 5.2.3), is between eight and twelve participants. Classes of this size are small enough to encourage good relations within the group yet large enough to provide sufficient variety and interest. All the learners play an active part, becoming participants rather than spectators.

5.1.6 The teaching team

The first-level courses are given by two teachers acting as animators who work closely together. We think it is important for the participants' sense of security that continuity is established by each animator performing the same role throughout the first three days. One will double and mirror (empathetic role), the second will present the exercises (structuring role). From the fourth day, the two animators can alternate according to their individual skills and preferences.

5.1.7 The psychological framework

One of the principal obstacles to learning is fear of appearing foolish or stupid, of not living up to the image one would like to present to the group. This fear is a barrier to successful self-expression. It is, therefore, important to give participants an empathetic framework within which they feel comfortable as they take their first public steps in the strange world of a foreign language. To achieve this, one has to create a climate of acceptance that will stimulate self-confidence, and encourage participants to experiment and to discover the target language, allowing themselves to take risks without feeling embarrassed. As they become more ready to make mistakes, they will gradually come to accept their strengths and weaknesses, and their self-confidence increases. We remove the emotional barriers and defences that stand in the way of learning so that they have confidence both in themselves and in how they speak the foreign language.

To be able to create an appropriate atmosphere and develop an empathetic attitude when working with learners, it is often necessary for the animators to undertake work on themselves, and we will deal with this aspect in the last two chapters.

5.2   First contacts with the language

Learning a language ... is not so much a matter of imitation as of individual re-creation. [AKOUN 1971: 302]

The methodological stages of LPD are deliberately precise from the very beginning of the course because we believe a well-defined framework helps learners to express themselves more freely; creativity needs the security of a framework in order to flourish.

We begin with exercises in which participants speak one at a time. Gradually, we progress to exercises which involve every member of the class. All the exercises make use of sequencing, in which participants practise the same theme several times, but on each occasion the context is changed—by switching masks, places, or roles in the first days, or by bringing in a new speaker or situation later. The participants' confidence and creativity increase as a result of the sequencing and at the same time their language skills develop.

Each main exercise: double, mirror, triadic relationships, etc. is preceded by a warm-up period which prepares the ground for the main exercise that follows. For best results, this warm-up period is sometimes presented in stages.

When the main exercise has been carried out several times, for example, when two or three participants have done the double exercise, we move on to an intermediate exercise. Some of these have a group function since they allow switching from individual to group activities, and this helps develop the group spirit. Others practise language acquisition skills, for example, the intermediate exercises presented in the mirror stage develop listening skills, the exercises on rhythm and expression help in recognizing and using the rhythms and melodies of the foreign language.

Sometimes the exercises can be included in traditional teaching programmes for exactly the same purposes. Some exercises will appear unusual to readers used to essentially verbal forms of teaching. Perhaps this applies to some warm-up exercises in particular. Although some suggestions will be offered regarding the purpose of these and other exercises, and the hypothesis on which they are based, it is not necessary to subscribe to these justifications fully in order to apply them in the classroom.

5.2.1 First step: doubling

Starting a course

After welcoming everyone and reminding them of the timetable, the animator explains the LPD approach using an image. Here is a hypothetical introduction:

> We're beginning a voyage into a foreign language; you will be entering that language one careful step at a time, in the company of the other members of your group. You will each travel at your own pace and the best way for you to make progress is to keep to your own pace. The trainers will respect your personal rhythm, whether you decide to go quickly or slowly. Though you will always have the company of others, when you voyage into the foreign language you must make your own way, on a road of your own choosing.

> During your voyage you will be discovering this new language; you can experiment to find out what is and what is not possible. Mistakes are necessary. The more you make, the better you will get to know the limits of the language and how to speak it. So, please, do make mistakes.

> We'll accompany each of you individually on your voyages, joining you wherever you are, whether you are at the beginning or some way down the road. In this way, we can work to meet your exact requirements.

> Don't aim too high, or look to see who is first past the post. For example, there are some tennis players who never really enjoy the game because they always compare themselves to a great international player, Aranxa Sánchez-Vicario or Stefan Edberg, or to the

best player in their club. But here in this group you are your own private reference point. Don't think in terms of reaching a specific point or learning fast but make your way carefully along your own path.

You will be living in direct contact with the language by using it. This is the best way to make it yours—just as we all learnt how to walk by walking.

We'll start by making contact with the most obvious characteristics of any foreign language: its rhythm and its melody. In this way, we can penetrate into the very heart of the language from the beginning.

This introduction demonstrates the personalized and experimental character of the LPD process. It prepares learners for a different view of themselves within that process. It invites everyone to accept themselves as they are, with their own character and individual style, which is an essential basis for self-confidence when learning.

We begin the day with a relaxation exercise. The animator explains that its essential purposes include increasing general awareness, concentration, and receptiveness (Chapter 3). Once the exercise is over, there is a feedback session in which participants can express their feelings; simple questions, for example, about the speed at which the exercise was conducted, the animator's voice, and so forth. These questions allow participants to speak to the group in their own language, to begin using their voices and expressing themselves in front of each other. At the same time, the animators can check how the relaxation was received and adapt as necessary to the characteristics of the group.

Warm-up exercise: the group mirror

Since adults, in particular, find it difficult to accept this type of exercise without understanding its purpose, the animator explains that we need to warm up before studying a language just as we do before taking part in a sport. For example, we have to use our muscles differently; the lips are not articulated in the same way and the gestures that accompany the language are also very different.

In this exercise the group forms a circle. When the animator makes a gesture, the participants reproduce the same gesture. When he or she makes a sound, or a series of words, they echo what was said. The series should be rich in onomatopoeia, alliterations, melodic variation, exclamation, and be accompanied by appropriate tones of voice and gestures. We appeal to sensory expression—smell, touch, sight, hearing—and we make extensive use of interjections and emotional expression, which capture the imagination and so help to improve memory as well as increase the group's use of emphasis in expression. This sequence provides an initial contact with the foreign language, with its rhythms, melodies, and sounds. Instead of being focused exclusively on meaning, the learners' attention is drawn to the prosodic features of the language. And the warm-up exercise prepares participants for the main exercise that follows.

Here is an illustration of the kind of group mirror activity described above. Each symbol / represents a choral response from the group.

The animator looks at some imaginary object in the centre of the room, such as a rose and speaks to it:

> Oh, how lovely you are! /
> Such lovely colours! /
> How pretty you are! /
> You are beautiful! /
> You are really beautiful! /
> Goodness, such colours! /
> That red! /
> That deep blood red! /

The animator pretends to hear a reply:

> What? /
> How? /
> What are you saying? /
> Ah, a rose! /
> You are a rose! /
> A rose! /
> That's a nice name! /
> It suits you! /

The animator goes up to the rose and smells it:

> Oh, how good! / You smell so good! /
> What a lovely scent! /
> How lovely you are! /
> How pretty you are! /
> What a lovely scent you have! /

The animator approaches as if to pick the rose:

> May I? /
> Eh? /
> What? You don't want me to? /
> Really, no? No? /
> What a pity! /
> I suppose you're right! /

The animator retreats gently:

> OK! /
> I have to go! /
> Bye for now! /
> Bye-bye! /
> See you soon!

The animator makes a gesture of parting while saying 'See you soon!'

One version of this exercise makes use of an imaginary nightingale which eventually flies away, promising to return to sing in the night; others feature a snail, an apple, a cat ...[1]

1 We owe this exercise to the French actor Jean-Christian Marcovici.

Main exercise: the double

The animator explains that each participant will be able to do the same as in the warm-up exercise, that is, to make contact with the sounds, rhythms, and melody of the foreign language—like a sculptor touching clay, holding it, kneading it, taking pleasure in feeling its consistency, before giving it shape.

A participant sits in front of the animator, both sitting in the same direction. We place a rug in this spot, a space where a learner can experiment with the foreign language. We call this the freedom rug, or 'the cloud of freedom'. The animator breathes in time with the learner and lets speech spring naturally from this rhythmical pattern.

At this point, it may be helpful to mention that the depth and pattern of a person's breathing is the biological basis of their physical, vocal, and verbal expression. The type of breathing is also a reflection of our emotional state. In adopting the same breathing pattern and, as far as possible, the same posture as the participant, the animator is to some extent assuming that person's physical characteristics. The animator does everything possible to empathize with the participant but expressing his or her sensations and aware that the participant's own perception may be different. We are not seeking telepathic communication in this exercise. As in everything we seek to do in LPD, what is most important is not the final result but the process. Although it might be ideal in theory for the animator to perceive and express exactly what the participant would like to say, our objective is to try to get on to the other person's wavelength, to feel empathy and so be *with* the other person.

The animator then becomes in some sense a spokesperson for the participant who lacks the words needed for communication. It should be repeated that the animator restricts these words to those which the participant might wish to say, given the necessary vocabulary. For example, if a participant feels tense but wants to hide their tension, the double would respect that and not reveal that feeling (as might happen in the use of psychodrama for therapeutic purposes).

The role of the animator is to bring participants into contact with the language, to make them feel it inside them, feel its rhymes and rhythms, melodies and sounds, and perhaps share the animator's affection for that language.

Returning to the LPD course, the animator introduces the masks and explains how they are to be used for protection, concentration, listening, etc. A participant sits in front of the animator and is given three masks, one after another.

Wearing the first of these, a whole mask, the participant as protagonist listens to a sequence of words spoken by the animator. This sequence is usually repeated so that it can be consolidated, and the protagonist becomes more familiar with the language used. Since the words are spoken spontaneously, this repetition is not verbatim, though it does keep more or less to the same order (Chapter 2: 2.3.1).

The second mask is referred to as the 'blind' half mask. Wearing this the protagonist is invited to speak in the target language, to practise its tones, rhythms, and melodies, as happened in the warm-up session. The animator returns to the same word sequence as before, adapting it as necessary in the light of what the protagonist says and how it is said—in other words, using whatever changes appeared in intonation, rhythm, in the omission of parts of the sequence, etc. These changes are useful signals which allow the animator to make adjustments to the presentation and content of the sequence.

If he or she wants to, the protagonist can see the rest of the group when wearing the third mask, a half mask with eye holes. We call it the 'seeing' half mask. The protagonist repeats the sequence of words spoken by the animator, which again is adapted according to how the protagonist reacted to the previous activity. At this stage, the protagonist's voice often becomes more assertive because it is being used almost as if he or she is addressing the others.

The word sequence is immediately repeated, again with minor changes, so curling back upon itself like a spiral.

The following examples are from an intensive weekend course:

Such calm, such mystery, such silence.
Doing nothing, waiting, listening in the dark,
no noise, not a word, not a sound.

I'm waiting for something to enjoy. There we go, slowly, calmly.

It's strange, I wonder what it will be like.
I'm there, I'm waiting, hearing, listening.
Sometimes it increases, sometimes it goes down again.
It changes, it's quite pleasant, it's melodious.

All the words are mixed up like colours in a big, big sentence.
I listen, I pay attention. I wait for the words to come, to mix themselves together.
They are all mixed. They are all colours, like a rainbow, light colours, dark colours.

It's like a wave, like the sea;
it comes in, it goes out, it comes back
and suddenly there's something in the way
and then it flows away,
it comes, it goes, it comes back again ...

At times this language refers to something real and immediate, at other times it stretches reality and turns it into poetry. So is born a language of impressions, sensations, and dreams, a poetic language which belongs to the body and the heart as well as the mind.

It may be helpful to consider this exercise from the two different perspectives of human relations and language.

Human relations
From the perspective of human relations, the double exercise corresponds to the bonding period we had during our first contact with the mother tongue, when we had a feeling of being an individual but bonded to another person, a physical osmosis that produces a strong mental resonance. This is the stage when the distinction between the real and the imaginary blurs and we tend to think only of the immediate, the here and now.

In the early stages of a course there is a tendency for classes to seek some common identity, to avoid any focus on what makes them different from each other, a form of self-defence when faced with the unknown. LPD responds initially to this need, which we also often feel when we meet someone for the first time.

At this stage, participants can feel particularly vulnerable. The double activity and the group exercises which accompany it help them to feel supported, so that they are relaxed about coming into contact with the foreign language. Human relations work largely on a basis of shared intuition and rhythm. The participants feel included. Even if there is little intellectual understanding of what the animator is saying, the animator and protagonist establish a form of reciprocal listening. Sometimes a synergy develops between them, a joining of forces where each gives the other strength.

Language

At this point, the language of 'I' begins to emerge. Through the impressions transmitted by individuals in the group, through their breathing, body attitudes, and in other subtle ways, they are the source and objective of the foreign language. The language they hear and respond to is individualized and unique. The participants live that language in a form of personal contact adapted to suit their own style. They receive the words spoken for them in time with their own rhythm. Symbolically, the animator transmits the soul of the foreign language to the participants.

The relaxation, mask, and double exercises help give expression to an inner language. This language is at first expressed for oneself, in the presence of others. Later on, during the third phase, when the 'seeing' half mask exercise is performed, the language may be addressed to the whole class, though the speaker may still prefer to keep his or her eyes closed. This reflects something we are familiar with from our childhood:

> Our inner language does not affect anyone and is not intended to influence anyone else. The egocentric language of the child is not concerned about anyone else but will accept, and even seek out, the presence of someone else. (Richelle 1976: 126)

In everyday life, speech is used first to hear oneself, and only then to make oneself understood by others. In the same way, participants begin by expressing ideas to themselves, as a necessary step in communicating with others. Language begins as a means of self-expression and self-communication; communication with other people comes later.

The participant, being close to the animator acting as a double, can hear every nuance of the foreign language during the exercise. The use of masks encourages a focus on the language's speech patterns; the ear, more than anything else, opens up the world of the foreign language.

Once in tune with the melody of the language, with its tonality, rhythms, and sounds, the participant begins what Jousse (1975) describes as a process of 'chewing on the language'. The sounds, words, and phrases are 'tasted' in the mouth; some feel strong, some weak. The participant, vibrating to its melodies and rhythms and 'tasting' its qualities, is carried away by the sheer physical pleasure of the language. To acquire a language this way is to do so by using precisely those elements which make it special so that it comes to feel less 'foreign'. The spoken language is experienced aesthetically, leading to a continued vocal and emotional resonance. Participants have, therefore, made contact with the substance before attempting to use or transform it. Even advanced participants, including teachers of the language who are not native speakers, benefit greatly from these exercises. Some have said that they feel in tune with the language's rhythms and melodies for the first time.

From the very beginning, participants are encouraged to be receptive to a relaxed and playful relationship with the language. They are able to progress with confidence, relaxing slowly into the language and letting themselves be carried away by its sounds and words.

Instead of simply imitating or repeating the language, participants reproduce it. We actually avoid the word 'repeat': there is far more to reproduction than simple repetition; it is the beginning of a process whereby the language is interiorized and appropriated. In fact, we often notice that participants do not reproduce anything, even when they are able to follow fully the sense of the words. But they do respond sensitively and can echo what the animator says, even making conscious or unconscious changes which are selected from what was said. These changes give direction to sequence; a sort of indirect dialogue begins to develop between animator and participant.

Sometimes participants come close to the sense as well as the tone of the message, through a process which is both intuitive and intellectual; thought probably owes more to 'resonance' than to 'reasoning'; they enjoy the sensation of what they hear, which leads them towards understanding. How a participant responds to listening will affect the meaning of a message. 'I am here, I'll wait', for instance, can imply both patience or impatience. The intonation used by the protagonist when reproducing these words may give a quite different impression from that which was originally intended, and the animator will pick it up in what he or she says next.

The aim of the double technique, like the mirror technique we are about to consider, is to give participants a foundation on which to build their own ways of expressing themselves. Later in the course, we can expand their knowledge using this foundation.

Intermediate exercise

After two or three participants have been protagonists, we switch to a period of group work. In the first few days, this would be concentrated on the language's rhythm and melody, possibly with the help of poems as in *Poetry and movement*. (Chapter 4: 4.3.2).

After each participant has performed the double exercises, and if there is time left at the end of the day, we invite anyone who is interested to experience a different version: *complementary doubles.*

Warm-up exercise: the echo in the mountain

This exercise is based on the principle of the group mirror. This time, however, the class is divided into several smaller groups which imagine themselves as a series of valleys. Each valley in succession echoes what the animator says. Changes in volume or rhythm take place in the valleys. The animator suggests short phrases which help the groups to repeat the echoes, for instance 'Oh, Oh!', 'I'm here!', 'I'm there!', 'I'm coming.', 'Gently.', 'Slowly.', and so on.

Main exercise: complementary doubles

A participant puts on the 'blind' half mask and becomes the protagonist with two animators sitting behind. One animator runs through a sequence (this corresponds to the first stages of the double exercise when the full mask was used). Then the sequence is repeated with the protagonist reproducing it at will. After the sequence has been given once more, the other animator can also join in, making adaptations according to observations of how the protagonist has responded to the sequence. The adaptation may complete, add to, or offer alternatives to, the words spoken by the other animator. Sometimes the second animator will remain silent throughout this stage, limiting his or her role to a symbolically supportive one by simply being present.

Continuing with the 'blind' half mask, the sequence is repeated once more. This time the class sits in a semicircle in front of the protagonist, echoing his or her words. Sometimes we ask half the class to sit in front of the protagonists and half behind, so creating a stereophonic effect. The resulting 'language bath' can have the effect of a 'verbal massage'.

In the last stage, using the 'seeing' half mask, the first animator and the protagonist return by themselves to the sequence. This time the protagonist responds alone, addressing the group.

This variation allows the other animator to enter into the role of double for the first time, his or her empathetic presence and speech complementing the first animator's more active role. In the echo stage, the other participants try to tune in to the protagonist. This immediately trains them to listen with special attention.

Intermediate exercise: exchanging first names

This exercise helps members of the group to make contact with each other and to exchange first names. We do not use this exercise until the second half of the day when the group has already made contact with each other to some extent. The interest of the participants in knowing each other's name is therefore greater and more specific.

The class stands in a circle while we explain that the first meaningful stage in any human contact is with the eyes. We then begin to make contact with each other in this way. When two people'e eyes meet, they walk towards each other, turn in a semicircle in the centre of the class, and walk backwards into the place where the other person was standing, still without looking away from each other's eyes. It may be suggested that some sort of gesture, or later on sound, be made when the two people meet in the centre.

The exercise continues but when two people meet at the centre they tell each other their names. After some time, the animator suggests that participants should not just say their names, but personalize how they say them, changing their intonation according to the person they meet.

Finally, we introduce the stage when two people's eyes meet and each has to say the other's name. They cannot change places until both names have been given. If A does not know B's name, they cannot change places but they can both exchange with others whose names they do know. A, for example, might hear B's name when B and F are exchanging, so if he wants to he can change places with B—but only if B knows A's name too.[2]

2 We owe this exercise to Laura Sheleen.

Using the double exercise in traditional teaching

The double technique can be a supporting role even in traditional teaching; when a student wants to say something but lacks the vocabulary, the teacher can stand behind him or her and provide the necessary language support. Working in this way has a quite different effect from working face to face. This supportive role can also be performed by other students.

We also use another exercise in which participants take turns to introduce one another. After a brief discussion in pairs to obtain the necessary information, one participant stands behind another, adopts that other person's identity and introduces him or her to the class. The person being introduced can correct or add to the information given. Presenting someone through role play in this way, with the presenter speaking on behalf of the partner, creates an entirely different impression from the more familiar style of introduction, the person being introduced transforming into an object of presentation.

Final stage

We generally end the first day with a poem accompanied by movement, as described in *Poetry and movement* (Chapter 4: 4.3.2), which prepares the way for the next day's technique: the mirror.

Integration

After each half day, we ask the class to lie down for two minutes, to find a relaxing position, close their eyes and simply open their minds to all the words, phrases, expressions in the foreign language they have heard during the day, or half day. This brief session allows them to fix some of the language material they have been hearing. It has the further advantage of marking the end of the session and providing the opportunity to return to oneself.

5.2.2   Second step: the mirror

The second day's work helps learners to listen more sensitively. We begin, as on every day, with a period of relaxation, followed by a warm-up exercise which prepares participants for the main activity: the mirror.

Warm-up exercises

Here are three examples of warm-up exercises. They can be used with classes which have different levels of energy or enthusiasm. Those not used for warm-up purposes can be used as intermediate exercises.

Imaginary masks

The class sits in a circle. The animator covers his face with his hands and turns to the participant on the left. The hands are gradually lowered to expose the face which is set in the expression of a mask. Then the animator pretends to take off this imaginary mask and give it to the person on the left who, while still looking at the animator puts it on, adopting the same facial expression. Like a mirror, the participant returns the visual image received.

Then the participant takes off the imaginary mask passed on by the animator, turns to the participant on the left and puts on another facial expression. Again, the next person takes it over as if it is a mask. When two or three participants have carried out this exercise, a sound is passed on with the mask, then a word, or phrase. This sound, word, or phrase has to be repeated by the next participant who is taking over the mask.

Mouth noises

The class sits in a circle. First, the animator makes a short series of vocal noises, for instance, clicking the tongue to a certain rhythm. The participant on the left repeats this sound sequence which is passed round the circle until the whole class has repeated it. Then it is the turn of the participant on the left to introduce a new series of sounds. After three or four sequences have been practised by the class, the next series of sounds is echoed by the class as a whole, followed by the next series, and so on. This produces a faster rhythm and a rapid change of expression.

Hand mirror

Participants stand facing each other and rub their hands together to increase their sensitivity. A raises his or her hands to shoulder height and B does the same, so that the palms of their hands are now opposite each other. A slowly makes a series of movements with the hands and B shadows the same movements as in a mirror image. Then B makes a series of hand movements for A to copy. Sounds can be added to the exercise, which are echoed by the person acting as mirror.

These exercises develop a person's ability to 'listen with the eyes', as well as providing practice for a number of non-verbal communication skills.

Main exercise: the mirror

In the earlier main exercise with masks, the animator listened to the protagonist but this time it is the protagonist who will listen. The animator takes the 'blind' half mask. A participant who is opposite adopts as nearly as possible the same position as the animator, puts on a similar mask and listens to what the animator says.

The animator concentrates and then expresses something which comes to mind spontaneously from the situation. In this way, he or she speaks personally and shares personal impressions and reactions to the present situation. The animator is focused on personal thoughts and feelings but does not forget the person opposite who is also wearing a 'blind' half mask. Sometimes this participant is included in the message. The message may be repeated a second time to consolidate it. Then the participant is invited to echo what was said by tuning in to the animator's voice, sharing its rhythm, nuances, and tones.

Afterwards, the participant changes places with the animator, and puts on a 'seeing' half mask. The animator, now without a mask, takes the participant's place. This time, the participant is not only

invited to echo the animator's voice but also to mirror gestures. This closer contact with the animator gives the learner an even better insight into the word sequence. The animator and participant repeat the sequence. The feeling of openness and rapport they come to share as a result of these activities will lead to improved dialogue between them in the later stages of the exercise.

In a new stage, animator and participant return to their original places and continue to sit facing each other, but now both have abandoned their masks. The participant is told that as well as continuing as mirror or echo, he or she can react at will, in other words, switch from the reproduction to the creation of dialogue.

The animator begins the same sequence, but now an elementary dialogue is emerging which has developed more or less from the participant's command of the language. The start of this dialogue can vary from the simple repetition of the animator's words, perhaps with varied intonation, to a more personal reaction from the participant such as 'Me too!':

Animator	I do like that.
Participant	(as echo) I do like that.
Animator	Oh, you do too! I *am* delighted! ...

On other occasions, the animator may be the one to open the way to a dialogue, possibly by introducing a point of difference or similarity:

Animator   Yes, but it's my first language.
Participant   It's not my first language.
Animator   No, it's *my* mother tongue, not yours ...

The animator establishes a difference or similarity and so encourages the participant to take a position and react to what is said. For the complete beginner, it is usually a question of being ready to take a risk by *reacting* rather than *responding*, which, in the fullest sense of the word, presupposes a more developed knowledge of the language. We shall deal with this later in the following day's class. In this final phase, especially when working with absolute beginners, the second animator sometimes acts as double behind the participant, ready to give support if required.

The rapport established between the animator and participant, and their combined efforts, produces a measurable level of mutual sensitive understanding. The level of communication achieved, then, depends on the empathetic relationship they have jointly created. This exercise reinforces the habit of inwardly listening and so understanding the speaker more clearly. This is an important habit, not just in order to learn a foreign language but in all communication.

Following the double exercise, which relates in part to 'fusion', the mirror exercise involves what might be called 'de-fusion'. It follows on from the points of difference expressed in the last phase of the exercise.

After the phase of echoing and mirroring the animator, and attempting an elementary dialogue, the participant realizes that the animator's 'Me' is not the same as the personal 'Me', that he or she is a separate person, not just different but uniquely so. It is the beginning of co-existence. The mirror exercise has begun the process of separating oneself from others, separating the real from the imaginary. We are preparing symbolically for a development which will be extended in *the triadic relationship* (Chapter 5: 5.2.3).

Intermediate exercise: a forest of sounds

This is an exercise in which members of the class work in pairs. In each pair, A creates a vocal sequence that lasts two or three seconds, based on the sound /ɔ:/. B repeats it until he or she is able to reproduce it faithfully. Each pair will have a different sequence of /ɔ:/ sounds. All the participants then spread out round the room. The person who is A in each pair closes his or her eyes and B repeats the agreed vocal sequence for A. At the same time, other pairs repeat their own /ɔ:/ sequences. A must recognize and find B in a forest of other /ɔ:/ sounds. When A comes close to B, B breaks off the sequence and A stops. B moves somewhere else in the room and repeats the /ɔ:/ sound. A again moves in B's direction. Finally, the animator tells all B participants to stand still and continue with their sequences until all the A participants have found them and formed pairs. The roles can then be reversed with B creating a sequence which A reproduces.

This exercise, taken from the tradition of personal development groups, heightens the listener's awareness of vocal nuances, including the characteristics unique to another person's voice.

After everyone has experienced the mirror activity, we devote the remaining time to a variation on it, for which the following exercise is a suitable warm-up.

Warm-up exercise: the gesture sequence

The animator begins by raising one hand in an opening movement from waist level to above the head. This gesture will constitute the basic movement for the exercise. This gesture is then extended spontaneously to create a gesture sequence of about two seconds. The participant on the left repeats the gesture sequence, and is followed in turn by the other members of the class, giving the impression of a waterfall. The participant on the left then repeats the original gesture but adds on a variation which is also repeated by the rest of the class. The animator asks the next participant to repeat the basic gesture and to prolong it accompanying it with a sound. The gesture and sound are taken up in mirror and echo by the whole class at the same time to speed up the rhythm of the exercise. Other participants create gesture and new sound sequences and after the fifth or sixth member has had a turn, the animator asks the next participant a word or phrase for the sound. Again, this is mirrored and echoed by the whole class.

Main exercise: the gesture sequence with words

The animator stands opposite and facing a participant acting as protagonist. The protagonist puts on the 'blind' half mask. Concentrating on the self, the participant allows a sequence of gestures to arise naturally. The idea is not to mime words or translate them into gestures, but to provide a physical accompaniment to the monologue going on in the mind.

We usually ask the protagonist to repeat the sequence of gestures once and then to accompany the gestures with whatever words or sounds come to mind. This exercise not only warms up the body, but also helps create favourable conditions for verbal expression.

The animator and the protagonist now change places. The animator has previously acted as echo and mirror. Now he or she tries to put the protagonist's sequence into words, expanding it linguistically. The protagonist echoes what comes closest to what he or she was trying to express, or whichever of the animator's suggestions is preferred. In the final stage of the exercise, the protagonist tries to express his or her sequence alone. The animator helps if necessary.

It has been noted that words were introduced by the animator in the previous double and mirror exercises, but in the gesture sequence here it is the participant who begins to create a personal verbal sequence. He becomes the author of his language.

From this stage onwards, all the word sequences will be created by the participants; animators will only help to formulate and extend these sequences, or make corrections to language where necessary.

Intermediate exercises: the 'first names' mirror activity

The class is divided into pairs facing each other. A in each pair slowly writes his or her name in the air with an index finger. B mirrors A. After several attempts, the exercise can be varied by A emphasizing a single letter, for instance, or writing more quickly, or using capitals. Then it is B's turn to write his or her name in the air.[3]

3 We owe this exercise to Laura Sheleen.

Using the mirror exercise in traditional teaching

All the warm-up and intermediate exercises in mirror activity are designed to improve listening skills and are, therefore, useful in traditional teaching. The mirror exercise can be performed between two students rather than between teacher and students, as follows:

The students sit in pairs facing each other. A tells B about something, for example, something that has happened; B has to try to repeat the information using the same gestures and tone of voice.

The exercise can also be carried out with three students, with B and C repeating A's information actions. Or, B and C could try to project not just what A said, but what they think was actually expressed, so underlining the essential elements of the message.

5.2.3 Third step: the triadic relationship

This stage takes place on the third day of an intensive course. After the usual relaxation exercise we suggest a warm-up activity which encourages self-expression.

Warm-up exercise: the imaginary object and the spontaneous gesture

Everyone sits in a circle. The animator pretends to pick something up from the floor and then gives this imaginary object or animal to the person on the left, who in turn passes it on to the next person, and so on until it comes back to the animator. Each member of the class then describes what was given and passed on. This first part of the warm-up exercise encourages concentration.

Next, the animator concentrates on his or her pelvis and breathing pattern, and spontaneously expresses whatever gesture, sound, word, or group of words comes to mind. This is picked up and repeated by the class as a whole. The person on the left then does the same, with a new gesture, sound, word, or group of words, which the class also repeats, and so on. It will be noted that this exercise has already been prepared for on the previous day, in the warm-up exercises for the mirror variation.

Main exercise: the triadic relationship

This exercise necessitates the presence of two animators. A participant is in the centre of the group with one animator (A) acting as double on the left, and the second animator (B) on the right. The protagonist puts on the 'blind' half mask, concentrates on his or her breathing and, as in the warm-up period, allows speech to emerge naturally. The sequence is repeated. Animator A acts as the principle double; when the words are presented for the first time he or she helps the protagonist to express himself or herself better, perhaps even to enlarge on what has been said. In this way, the repeated words are an extension of the first attempt. Animator B can help, for example, by highlighting any contrasting elements in the utterance or completing animator A's doubling.

The protagonist now puts on a 'seeing' half mask and repeats the sequence, while animator B gradually moves round to sit in front of the protagonist and starts a dialogue with the protagonist. Animator A continues to act as double and offers support and help with language difficulties.

Variation

During the final stage, we sometimes ask the protagonist to choose someone else from the group to act as an interlocutor for the word sequence. In this situation, animator B acts as double for the second participant. We usually try this variation only at the end of the day, or when the protagonist is able to speak confidently, because although animator B's intervention is attuned to the protagonist's ability, the same may not be true for another participant. When the course is held over several weekends, this variation may be used on day one of the second weekend, since it prepares for a meeting between the two participants the next day, *the deferred encounter* (Chapter 5: 5.2.4).

Another variation is a triangular exercise: animator A leaves his or her position as double and sits facing the protagonist, to the left. Both animators begin to talk with him or her and both animators can give the protagonist any support needed.

The careful transition from the situation when participants and animators depend on each other, to the point when protagonists become autonomous, should now be obvious. The participants are by now already setting the theme of the word sequence; instead of simply reacting to dialogues set by the teacher, they are beginning to make genuine contributions which have meaning for themselves. To the principle that speaking is pleasurable, which dominates the mutual relationship between protagonist and animator, is added the principle of speaking with a purpose with the support and intervention of the animator. The playful language used in the earlier double and mirror exercises now becomes utilitarian language. Animator B, in the role of supporter and helper, links the relationship in the classroom to the world outside; a link between what is imagined, represented in the mirror and the double, and the reality, which the animator represents when offering help. Animator B also begins or reinforces a process in which participants become more open towards other members of the group. This opening-up process continues in the variations described above and will be continued in the stages that follow. So, each participant begins to feel ready to take responsibility for what he or she says. We are familiar with this development from our own childhoods:

In the mother–child relationship it is not yet possible to talk of dialogue since there is no choice of object. Exchange or dialogue requires the intervention of a third person. This third person, whoever it may be, is needed to take the child out of its closeted relationship with its mother in order to give the dialogue life in terms of language, that is, symbolically. (Lemoine 1972)

Teachers who often initiate dialogues by asking questions about 'you' to which they already know the answer, find it difficult to teach this LPD step, in which the dialogue depends on each individual's point of view, in other words, on how each person involved in the conversation expresses their 'me'. In LPD, the animator must react to the participant's point of view and so define his or her response accordingly as a person with feelings and interests and not just as a conveyer of information.

Let us take a simple example: if a learner were to say 'I like travelling', and the teacher asked 'Why do you like travelling?', the nature of the question requires a particular type of response from the student. So the content and direction taken by the dialogue are controlled by the teacher. Any student without the necessary vocabulary to attempt a reply is in a difficult position. In LPD, when a participant says 'I like travelling', an animator expresses a personal point of view such as 'Me too, I like travelling a lot', or perhaps 'Personally, I don't like it much', or 'Sometimes I'm a bit nervous when I go abroad. I like travelling but at the same time it scares me a little'. In this way, the protagonist is free to make a genuine response which might be to follow the animator's lead but could just as well be to pursue a different line altogether.

In LPD, everyone involved in a discussion gives an individual and personal response to the topic of conversation. There is now dialogue in the true sense of the word, a meeting between two people who express their own points of view, their differences, and their similarities.

Using the triadic relationship in traditional teaching

The need for two teachers makes it difficult to adapt this particular exercise. But teachers trained by us who subsequently work in a more traditional setting take with them the principle of developing a true dialogue. Instead of asking rhetorical questions, they try to express their own points of view and so encourage their students to do the same. This means replacing the 'What is this ...?', 'Why ...?', and 'How ...?' questions with comments beginning 'Personally, I ...', and encouraging the open relationships among their students which will encourage everyone to say what they really think.

5.2.4 Fourth step: the deferred encounter

All of the following exercises are suitable for use in a traditional language teaching context. The *deferred encounter* normally takes place on day four of an intensive course. In this exercise, two participants will work out a spontaneous sequence which serves to start off a dialogue between them. First, we will look at the warm-up exercise which symbolically introduces the postponed dialogue activity.

Warm-up exercise: tambourine rhythm

The class sits in a circle. The animator takes a tambourine, concentrates for a moment on his or her breathing rhythm and then strikes the tambourine in order to express personal feelings using rhythm. The other members of the class pick up the rhythm and clap in time with the animator. The tambourine is then passed to the left and that participant creates a new rhythm for everyone to imitate, and so on until the tambourine has been right round the group. After this process of tuning-in to tambourine rhythms, there are two possible extensions, *The conductors*, and *West Side* (Chapter 4: 4.2.1).

Main exercise: the deferred encounter

In this exercise the class divides into two, with one half at each end of the room. Two protagonists (one from each group) present unprepared sequences and then work with the animators to extend and improve them. The two protagonists then meet in the centre of the room. It is worth noting that this exercise parallels an everyday situation where two people who live entirely different lives meet and their encounter gives rise to dialogue. The other participants form a semicircle behind the protagonist from their particular group, who creates a dialogue with the other protagonist, with the support of an animator. This coming together of the two-word sequences leads to a third, sometimes made by mixing up equal parts of the first two, but at other times drawing more heavily from one sequence than the other.

After their sequences have been heard for the first time, we ask the two protagonists to stand some distance apart and imagine that there is a curtain between them. An animator now stands behind each protagonist and 'recharges' that person's part of the dialogue. To do this, each protagonist says the first phrase or two of his or her dialogue which is developed by his or her animator as far as the protagonist's present knowledge of the language permits. Members of each group listen carefully. Each protagonist echoes whatever part of this new sequence coincides with what he or she is trying to say. This stage could be compared to listening-in to a telephone conversation but hearing only one of the two speakers. This stage gives each protagonist the language needed to cope with the next step.

The protagonists meet again and repeat their dialogue but this time members of their groups are ready to give any help they might need. The animators stand further back, ready to intervene if required but preferring to let the protagonists express themselves without prompting unless it is from their group.

This exercise enables participants to enter into conversation with one another for the first time. The fact that the encounter is 'deferred' means that the protagonists, especially beginners, can prepare what they are going to say when the dialogue is repeated. There are advantages, too, for more advanced learners since they can improve the fluency of their speech and add different shades of meaning and expression.

5.2.5 Fifth step: the direct encounter

This time, the protagonists meet without having prepared their sequences in advance. To some extent we make things easier by asking them to take up opposed positions, one saying 'Yes', the other 'No'. By so doing, we appeal to two basic dramatic devices, one expressing desire, the other opposition. But first we lead up to this activity with a warm-up exercise which focuses on these two positions.

Warm-up exercise: yes-no, me-you

We tell the participants that they will be using language made up of just four words: 'Yes', 'No', 'Me', 'You'. We invite them to walk around the room and, using just those four words, to make contact with other participants. The dialogues which result depend very heavily, of course, on varied intonation. We ask them to then extend their dialogue, expressing whatever comes to mind spontaneously, but beginning with some of the four words. Mini-dialogues begin to occur.

Main exercise: the direct encounter

The animators sit opposite each other in the centre of the class, about two metres apart. Two protagonists take up sitting positions between them, each with their back to one of the animators. The remainder of the class divides into two, half sitting behind one of the protagonists, and half behind the other.

The meeting between the two protagonists follows the pattern of the warm-up exercise. One starts to speak, pronouncing the word 'Yes' in a variety of different intonations, the other uses the word 'No', both gradually adding whatever other words happen to suggest themselves, and so starting a dialogue.

These initial 'Yes' and 'No' dialogues help learners to feel more at ease in conversation and more ready to express themselves spontaneously. Animators are there to supply any words needed to express their thoughts. The dialogue is usually repeated a second time to consolidate it.

In line with the method in the *deferred encounter* above, a 'recharge' of each protagonist then takes place using the curtain technique.

In the next step, each protagonist enters into a conversation with an animator; A talks to B's animator (who acts B's role) and B talks to A's animator (who acts A's role). The situation approximates to experiences outside the classroom when learners talk to friendly native speakers (see picture above).

In the final step, the protagonists meet again, but on this occasion each group provides support. The animators are some distance away but ready to intervene should the need arise.

When the exercise has been practised twice, we ask the participants to choose for themselves opposites like 'Yes' and 'No' which will help them to express themselves more readily, for example, black–white, day–night, etc.

5.3   Further stages

We can consider the five parts discussed so far as representing progression on an interpersonal level. After the first three individualized steps, in which one participant is the centre of the process, there is a gradual progression towards encounters with other group members. This is prepared in the fourth step and carried out directly in the fifth.

At the end of the five steps, different paths are open to animators depending on the make-up and character of the classes. We set out below some of the techniques available to them.

5.3.1   Dialogue without words

This exercise involves an encounter between two protagonists who communicate by using gesture rather than sound. We sometimes use this technique at the beginning of the second week of two-week courses to help participants to readjust after their day off. We also use it the same week in conjunction with *Meeting through photo people* to be described later in this chapter (Chapter 5: 5.3.3). On intensive weekend courses, this exercise can also be used at the beginning of the third weekend.

Warm-up exercises

We use one of the following exercises, depending on the group.

Tambourine dialogue
A participant taps out a rhythm on a tambourine which is picked up by the rest of the class clapping their hands. The tambourine is passed round so that everyone takes a turn. When the tambourine comes back to the animator, he or she keeps it and gives a second one to a participant standing opposite. A short 'dialogue' between the two tambourines takes place, after which the tambourines are passed to the left, and the process is repeated.

This exercise not only prepares participants for the exercise that comes later, but makes them more aware of the possibilities of communication without words.

The dynamic tableau
Participant A comes to the centre of the room and adopts a particular pose, for example, holding out one hand as if to give somebody something. Participant B adopts a complementary pose, in this case, reaching out as if to receive something. A then moves away. His or her place is taken by C who adopts a complementary pose to that of B, who then moves away and is replaced by D, and so on.

The meaning of the shared poses changes with each new participant since a new pose will usually produce a new situation. The exercise is a form of silent body language between participants.[4]

4 We owe this exercise to Augusto Boal.

Main exercise: dialogue without words

In this exercise, the class divides into two and a protagonist from each group comes to the centre and meets a protagonist from the other group, face to face; they enact a silent dialogue during which what they want to express is displayed by their gestures.

They then separate in order to prepare the same dialogue in words with the help of an animator and their group. They then return to have a spoken dialogue with the other protagonist. This exercise can be extended by asking the two protagonists to choose others to take their place (*relay technique*). The topic changes according to the wishes of the new protagonists.

Provided there is no risk from the class's point of view of carrying on the exercise for too long, it is sometimes possible to bring together an original protagonist with the person who took over from their partner. This gives rise to a new dialogue in which the language is often much richer than before because of the dialogues that took place earlier.

Intermediate exercise

We continue our work on the language's rhythm and melody using poetry (Chapter 4). We also make use of the following exercise.

Talking thumbs

The class divides into pairs. Everyone makes a fist with their right hand, then raises the right thumb and uses it to open a conversation with their partner. To begin with, the 'conversation' may take place in silence and focus on the movements of the thumbs. Soon the whole body takes part and words often gradually come in of their own accord.

5.3.2   Cushions

This exercise enables the group to pass from a state of individual reality or imagination to that of the whole class. This exercise sometimes results in strongly symbolic activity within the class; all the participants become responsible for the characters they create. This not only helps to establish the identity of the protagonists who represent these characters but also encourages all the participants to help each other.

Warm-up exercise: tit for tat

The participants stand in two lines, A and B, back to back. On a sound from the tambourine, everyone in line A turns round and adopts a particular pose. When the tambourine sounds again, everyone in line B turns round and adopts a complementary pose to that of his or her partner in line A. For example, if one participant holds out a hand, a partner can do the same or adopt a pose of refusal. On a double sound from the tambourine, the groups turn away from each other and one participant at the end of line A goes to the other end of the same line, thereby changing the partnerships between the lines. This is repeated at each stage in the exercise to ensure a series of new partners.

At a new signal from the animator, members of line B turn round again, and adopt new poses. At a second signal, members of line A turn round and respond to the pose of their opposite partner.

When this exercise has been successfully introduced, variations are possible: movement can be introduced in slow motion in time to the tambourine, or sounds can be added to the movement, or the exercise can end with a short discussion between those taking part.

Main exercise: creation of imaginary characters on cushions

The class divides into two groups, each with its own animator. In the middle of each group is a cushion, and the group has to imagine that someone is sitting on the cushion and to decide who that person is. There is only one rule: the first suggestion must always be accepted; if one participant says there is a man on the cushion, no one can say it is a woman, or if someone says the person is twenty years old, no one can make him younger or older. The group then puts together a description of the imaginary person.

Sometimes, when the groups have described their imaginary person in some detail, we tell them that the person will have to carry out a project. They must decide what the project should be, and they should bear in mind that a second person will be needed to help in the task. All this prepares the group psychologically for the encounter that follows.

We then invite each group to choose a representative to take the place of the imaginary person they have created, and to sit on the cushion. In performing this role, each representative of an imaginary person will be meeting the other group's imaginary person. The two cushions are placed in the middle of the room and the representatives sit down on them. Before they begin a conversation they agree where to meet, in a park, café, waiting room, or a cloud ... They must also agree on the time of the meeting. (This gives a time and space framework to the activity.)

Helped by their groups and animators, the two protagonists now begin to talk together. A 'recharge' session immediately afterwards reinforces and extends their sequence as for *The deferred encounter* (5: 5.2.4).

The sequence can either be followed by a second meeting of the two imaginary characters or by an adapted version in which each of them meets a member of the other person's group (*cross-over technique*). Provided the group dynamics are favourable, this development can be carried a stage further with each protagonist meeting two, then three, new participants at the same time. Finally, the two imaginary characters may meet for a last time. Be careful, because they may be too tired!

Variations

After the identity of the two imaginary characters has been established, instead of selecting just two participants from a group to impersonate them, the class is divided into pairs of members from the original two groups, so that everyone can take part in the role play. Membership of the pairs can be rotated with the animators going from one to the next to provide language assistance when asked. Finally, two participants volunteer to meet in front of everyone. One represents the imaginary person from group A, the other the imaginary person from group B. If necessary, they can be supported by the other members of their respective groups.

Sometimes, after the identity of two imaginary characters has been established, we ask three members of group A to take the part of journalists and interview one of these imaginary characters in group B, who is again supported by the remaining members of the same group. This technique is described in the following section.

5.3.3 Meeting through photo people

We usually introduce this technique at the beginning of the second week and use it to touch on the issue of social roles in preparation for the mythical roles to be discussed in Chapter 6.

Warm-up exercise: metamorphoses

We ask the participants to spread out and try walking in different ways, for example, as if they were in a great hurry or as if they had all the time in the world. They can walk on sand or rocks and feel their feet in touch with the ground. They can imagine themselves as young, middle-aged, or old, as clowns or shepherds, as showing cunning, pride, or fear. The possibilities are endless. We sometimes ask them to talk to each other in brief encounters. This warm-up session lets them consider in detail various types of character and it stimulates their bodies as well as their imaginations.

Main exercise: meeting of the photo people

We spread out twenty or so pictures on the floor taken from magazines, catalogues, etc. They show people looking and behaving in different ways. We ask participants to choose one of the pictures and remember it but without saying which. *Dialogue without words* (5.3.1) would be a useful way to exploit this situation if it has not already been used.

Participants would be asked to act out a silent dialogue in the manner of a character in one of the pictures. But we can also use a new exercise that concerns an interview with a person in a picture.

Two protagonists who have been characters from the pictures go to opposite parts of the room. The class divides into two groups. In each group three participants act as journalists to interview one protagonist of the other group while the others in the group support him as doubles. This technique will give more depth to the characters of the 'photo people' whose personalities are gradually filled out in response to the journalists' questions. Each group has an animator in support. Sometimes, as for the imaginary people in *Cushions* (5.3.2), we suggest that the 'photo people' have some wish or project which will require someone else's help.

The journalists can pass on information about what they have found out to the protagonist of the other group. Alternatively, we can pass directly to the following stage.

We invite the two protagonists to come to the centre of the room and then ask them to agree on a place and time to meet. They now imagine that they meet and begin to talk together. At this point, we decide which language techniques will be most useful to help this particular class to consolidate and develop the language acquired so far.

We often follow on with an exercise in which the two protagonists reverse roles and meet once more. This can increase each person's awareness of another's point of view and their powers of expression. They then go back to their original roles. We usually suggest that this final encounter should last no more than five minutes, often with the effect of shortening the sequence and stimulating faster dialogue. The protagonists then leave their roles as characters from the pictures and return to being themselves.

Variation: the confidants

Sometimes, instead of using the interview and role-reversal exercises, we ask the protagonists to choose a 'confidant' from their group. Later, there can be opportunities for cross-over arrangements: protagonist A meets B's confidant, for example; B's confidant then tells

protagonist B about the meeting with A, and so on. This helps to
develop a command of reported speech as in real journalism. Finally,
the two protagonists meet again, with their confidants in support.

Written activity

The journalists can be asked to write a report on what they found
out, and at the same time the protagonists and their supporters can
write about the information they passed on. Comparing these
reports afterwards can lead to a fruitful discussion.

Apart from the earlier exercise involving poetry, this is the first
time in the course that outside visual aids, pictures, and writing
materials, have been used. The 'photo people' activity involves participants in a social world. It may include stereotypes but it excites
their imaginations none the less. In the next chapter, we enter the
world of psychodramatic roles which have their origin in a deeper
level of the imagination.

5.4 Dramatization

Most sessions described so far start with two people and gradually
expand to include the whole class. We are now going to present some
techniques needed for involving the whole class in putting on a play.
This calls for a great deal of confidence on the part of the participants,
both in themselves and in each other, since they will expose their
strengths and weaknesses more than before. For this reason, we do
not make use of these techniques until well on in the course. Here are
some examples.

5.4.1 Fahrenheit 451

Truffaut's film *Fahrenheit 451* is about a totalitarian state that burns
all books—451°F being the temperature at which paper ignites. At the
end of the film, people are seen walking in the countryside, each
reciting a literary work which they have learnt by heart. That scene
provides the starting-point for the following exercise.

Main exercise

Participants spread out round the room. They have to imagine that
they are walking in the countryside somewhere they enjoy. They walk
at what they feel to be a suitable pace for the sort of landscape they
have in mind. They should think of a sentence in the foreign lan-

guage and repeat it to themselves, inwardly to begin with, but then to anyone they come across as they walk around the room. Animators should provide language support. They should repeat the sentence first as a whisper and then out loud, varying the intonation. Some of the dialogues which result can be highly surreal. After a while, the participants should stop and let us hear their sentences individually. Then, the whole class forms a circle in the middle to repeat the mini-dialogues they liked best when they were walking around the room. The class chooses two of the sentences to use as a mini-dialogue in the next activity.

Two types of dramatization can be used to follow this activity:

The rapporteur

The class divides into two. Helped by an animator, each half prepares a dramatized scene using the two sentences chosen as a mini-dialogue. Although it is possible to perform the two scenes one after another, we have tried a different approach.

A person from each group is asked to observe the other group's scene as it is played and then describe it to their own group who now perform it. The groups then perform their own scenes. In this way, two versions of each scene are played, making four versions in all:

1 Group A's scene is played by group B according to their observer's report.
2 Group A's scene is played by group A.
3 Group B's scene is played by group A according to their observer's report.
4 Group B's scene is played by group B.

Animators who want to introduce a written activity at this stage could ask the groups to prepare scripts for versions 1 and 3 based on the reports made by the observers.

The theatre forum

The basic idea is for the participants to perform a short play using the two chosen sentences with an ending of which the audience does not approve. After deciding which sentences they want to keep from the *Fahrenheit 451* exercise, the two groups, working separately and with an animator to help, prepare two short plays with unsatisfactory endings. Group A presents its play. The play is performed again but this time a member of group B who disapproves of the ending is allowed to say 'Stop!', at which point the actors 'freeze'. The person who stopped the performance takes over from one of the actors and improvises a new direction for the play. The play can be stopped again by another member of group B who has a new idea for an ending, and so on. A similar sequence occurs when group B presents its play.

This technique achieves one of the objectives of the sequences, which is to use the language in a variety of ways to progressively develop expression.[5]

5 The theatre-forum technique was devised by Augusto Boal.

5.4.2 The chairs

Main exercise

Chairs are placed in deliberate positions in the middle of the room, for example, two chairs close together and facing one another. The arrangement creates a surface onto which participants can project their imaginations.

The class makes suggestions about what drama the chairs could represent, for example, a couple with a lawyer, a student at a job interview, people in a queue. One participant takes notes and afterwards the list of suggestions is read out. Votes are taken to decide which suggestion should be acted out; no one is allowed to vote for their own idea. The class then makes a final choice between the two most popular suggestions. They divide into groups of three to rehearse independent versions of the same story. Animators provide help when asked. Everyone comes together again to watch the performances.

The activity can be extended by creating new settings, for example, by giving one of the chairs to a member of the other group. A new dialogue emerges and this helps to develop and broaden language acquisition.

Variation

Before the participants come in the room chairs are arranged in different settings, some in groups of three or four, others in pairs, side by side, facing each other, and so on. Participants sit on the chairs and let new ideas for plays arise from their feelings and imaginings about the arrangement of the chairs.[6]

6 We owe the variation of this exercise to Marie Dufeu.

5.4.3 Dramatization of tableaux vivants

Several techniques used in drama teaching can be adapted for language teaching. Two examples are given below.

The sculpture

The class divides into two groups. Participant A transforms another participant, B, in the same group, into a sculpture, that is, A puts B into a pose from which he or she must not move. Participant C does the same with D in the other group. The two 'sculptures', B and D, are brought face to face. It is also possible for each group to divide into smaller groups who then make a 'sculpture' in the same way. The 'sculptures' are given a word or phrase by members of their group. Animators are available to help. At a signal, the 'sculptures' come alive and repeat the given word or phrase adopting different tones of voice. They then begin a dialogue which starts with the same words.

The tableau vivant

One of the participants adopts a pose in the centre of the class. A second participant joins in, then a third. After several people have taken up positions to complete the tableau, the other participants are asked to create a scene around the most important characters represented and to decide upon a title for the tableau. At a signal, the figures come alive and begin to talk.

Variation

Another possibility starts with the participants spreading out round the room. At a signal, for example a clap, everyone freezes where they are, after which another signal allows them to make one movement towards other participants. As this activity continues, three or four smaller groups are created, and the activities described above can be performed.

5.4.4 The pyramid

The class is divided into pairs and each person describes to the other something that has happened to them. Animators provide help when asked. Each pair then chooses which of the stories it wants to tell. The pairs join to make groups of four, and the two previously chosen stories are told for the second time. One of these stories is chosen to repeat and the groups of four are joined together into units of six or eight, depending on the overall numbers in the class. The selected stories are then told again. At this point, each group can be asked to write down the story they have chosen. The last two stories are told to the class as a whole. A vote is taken on which story should be

7 We are grateful to Ken Sprague, British psycho-dramatist and story-teller, for this activity.

performed. This approach has two advantages; the play has its origins in one of the class members, and everyone has been involved in the selection process. The person who suggested the original story then stage manages a performance using a cast selected from the class.[7]

5.4.5   Role play

Role play is used in LPD, but in the tradition of the person who created this technique and psychodrama, Jacob Levy Moreno. Using certain setting techniques (Dufeu 1983b, 1990), we make sure that the characters are imaginatively and productively chosen.

These role plays are sometimes created out of an activity using some other form of expression. For example, drawings by participants can be used as stage designs or character descriptions. In this way, the play develops using imaginative ideas from several participants.

5.5   Art and psychodramaturgy

LPD is still a novice in this area of expression but the reactions so far of those taking part encourage us to continue. We have used art to stimulate participants' imaginations. Symbolism in many paintings can have a particularly strong appeal to self-expression.

5.5.1   Dramatization of surrealist tableaux

Warm-up exercise: back-to-back dialogue

Participants sit in pairs with their backs to each other, saying what-ever comes into their minds. After four or five minutes of conversa-tion, they change partners.

Main exercises

Here are two exercises based on works by the Belgian surrealist painter René Magritte.

The meeting
The schoolmaster and the evening gown is a work which consists of two paintings presented together. One shows a man in a black suit seen from behind and wearing a bowler hat, the other a nude with long hair, also seen from behind. The moon can be seen above the head of each figure.

Two groups are formed. In one group, participant A takes the role in the painting of the man's moon, facing a group of 'men' (in fact comprising men and women) who represent the man in the bowler hat. In the other group, participant B plays the role of the woman's moon, facing a group of 'women' (also a mixed group) who represent the nude. A dialogue takes place within each group between the moon and its respective group members. The man's moon then meets the other group representing the nude, and the woman's moon meets the group representing the man in the bowler hat. There follows a meeting between one 'man' and one 'nude', with members of their respective groups acting as doubles. Finally, the class divides into pairs, one representative of the 'man' meets one of the 'nude'.

Using the stimulus of the paintings and their strong images, the imaginative input from within the class tends to be very fruitful and often results in a great deal of language use.

I am important
The month of the grape-harvest is a painting which represents a group of men standing outside a house. At first glance, they are all very similar in appearance, wearing bowler hats, blue coats, white shirts, and red cravats. They are looking through a window into a room of which all that can be seen is a blue wall, yet at the same time they are also looking towards the person looking at the painting.

In a recent course, participants were asked to look carefully at this painting and decide where they might fit in, that is to say, which figure they identified with. They were then asked to place themselves in the frame of a 'window' which I had marked on the floor with two scarves. Each person was asked to say one sentence in that position. Again, animators provided help when asked. Afterwards, the class discussed which of the sentences held most meaning for them. They remembered three in particular: 'I am important', 'My future is ahead of me', and 'I can see nothing but nobody can see me either'. These three sentences were the starting-point for scenes acted out by the participants. The painting had become a spring-board to a new topic which was created from within the class.

We are currently planning to experiment further with abstract paintings, in particular, with work by the Chinese abstract painter Zao Wou-Ki. His paintings express an ephemeral energy, a drawing together of forces which can be used to form the basis of ideas for dramatic interpretation.

5.6   Back to reality

We generally conclude our two-week courses with a return to the
more familiar reality of day-to-day living. Participants who have
been enriched by the power of their imaginations are helped to use
their experiences to exercise more control over their everyday lives.
We shall leave aside for the moment techniques using fairy-tales and
myth which are described in the next chapter. The following forms a
typical ending to an elementary two-week course.

Main exercise: difficult situations in a foreign country

Towards the end of the course, in order to make a direct connection
with the outside world, we sometimes ask participants to talk about
situations they have found, or might find, difficult during their time
in a foreign country.

One class had run into problems using the telephone. Participants
proposed acting out the difficulty with an animator playing the role
of an antagonistic office worker or telephone operator, impatient
when he or she was not understood, and given to making bad-tem-
pered remarks. A second animator acted as double to help the participants acting the situation. These dramas were repeated several
times until participants felt able to perform them on their own.

Another class chose situations which included a restaurant with a
menu for foreigners whose prices were different from those advertised outside; a train journey when a ticket collector was unpleasant
to a participant who could not find her ticket; and a stay with a local
family that had gone disastrously wrong. In this class, the situations
were oriented towards the past and their real-life experiences. At the
same time, since the situations were re-enacted by those who had
experienced them, participants were able to express some of the
frustrations they had felt at the time. Being able to relive a bad
experience and to have more linguistic control over it was found to
be very beneficial.

5.7   Further work

Returning to the real world brings us to one of the possible ways for
continuing LPD after this first course.

Complete beginners repeat the two-week course in order to
broaden and deepen their knowledge and experience of the target
language.

There are two options open to false beginners and those who are further advanced. The first is directed towards a general improvement of skills. Depending on the needs of the individual student, we would focus on studying and performing written texts chosen according to the dramaturgical principles outlined in Chapters 1 and 7. Alternatively, we extend the direction of role play and creative techniques in order to broaden participants' contact with the target language.

The second option is to concentrate on training participants in the context of roles which are important to them in their professional lives. The method continues to include the following techniques; recharge, cross-over, role-reversal, and relay, which have been described in this chapter and are also covered in the next one. Such techniques allow for a deepening and broadening of the language. They often involve the use of video which allows work to be carried out on both language and behaviour strategies.

5.8 Conclusion

The techniques described in this chapter are a system of LPD procedures which are continuously adapted by our animators to suit the needs of each new class. Since LPD is at the service of participants' self-expression, it requires a great deal of flexibility on the part of the animators. While there is a common thread to our work and certain principles must be observed, LPD is in a state of constant evolution.

Each new course provides an opportunity to create new exercises and leads to fresh insights. We therefore seek the roots of a problem in our own attitudes and actions rather than in the participants. Was the presentation satisfactory or the technique adapted to suit the group? Did we take one stage in the exercise too quickly? What should we have done differently? We are sometimes made aware of our limitations and forced to accept them, but at the same time, we are invited to overcome them. The theory and practice of LPD are not developed through our work with groups alone but are also related to our own personal development and our understanding of what communication is. Clearly, there is still much work to be done.

Intensive course

Stage one

	Type of work	Technique
Week 1	Individual or group	Doubling The mirror The triadic relationship
	Meeting others	The deferred encounter The direct encounter Dialogue without words Cushions
Week 2	Meeting the imaginary	Meeting through photo people Fahrenheit 451 Théâtre forum The rapporteur The chairs Tableaux vivants The pyramid Role play Surrealist tableaux
	Back to reality	Difficult situations in a foreign country

Absolute beginners retake Stage one before beginning Stage two.

Stage two

	Type of work	Technique
Week 3 *and further weeks*	General enlarging and improving of language	Drama techniques Drama texts Creative work
	or Functional work relating to specific professional situations	Training in role play (recharge, cross-over, role-reversal, relay)

FIGURE 8 *Technical stages in linguistic psychodramaturgy (LPD)*

6 Fairy-tales and myth in LPD

Reality is our indispensable fairy-tale. [AUSLÄNDER]

6.1 Functions of fairy-tales and myth

Since the reasons for using fairy-tales and myth in language teaching may not be immediately obvious to some teachers, it is worth beginning by describing the functions for which these two forms of expression are used in LPD.

In Chapter 5, we examined several activities which stimulate our imaginations, including *Imaginary masks* (5.2.2), *Cushions* (5.3.2), *Meeting through photo people* (5.3.3), *Fahrenheit 451* (5.4.1). But there is another invaluable source for expression in a foreign language: fairy-tales and myth.

First, fairy-tales and myth represent a means of contact with the deep sources of our imagination. We each carry an imaginary world within us, and fairy-tales and myth provide a 'drawbridge' that connects us with that inner symbolic universe. To some extent, we are able to rediscover our childhood sense of a mythical, magical world, where the imaginary can roam freely. At the same time, we come into direct contact with our unconscious. We can return to the sources of our deepest being, even, perhaps to the expression of its origins, full of images, symbols, and magic. We can touch the inner reality where the sources of our ego and latent talents lie hidden. We can, in this way, connect with the roots of our being.

Consider Jung's view that 'myths and symbol are the most archaic structures of the psychic life' (Eliade 1976: 16) and are created by the (collective) unconscious. Myths are, therefore, an unrivalled expression of our inner thoughts and form crucial bridges between all our experiences of living.

Fairy-tales and myth can also perform a revelatory function, and can mould the expression of a message beyond the words used to conceal or convey it. They often translate events or thoughts we experience, but fail to understand, into images. In this way, they help us to identify that experience. We find in gods, princes, heroes, and beggars the symbols of our primordial needs, of our desires, our fears, and private unrest.

Fairy-tales and myth can have a structuring function. In LPD, the use of myth involves a twofold movement. On the one hand, a participant projects a certain dynamic from his or her own inner self onto the myth; this naturally influences his or her reading of it and its impact. On the other hand, myth produces its own psychic effect on the participant.

In the same way, we project our emotional selves when we take on a character in a fairy-tale, but the particular features of that character carry us towards certain types of action and relationship. We are witnessing a twofold creative relationship.

Fairy-tales and myth can affect the quality of the group as a whole. Cohesion within the group is generally strengthened through contact with the imaginary world which represents and expresses both the emotive quality of the group and the emotional qualities of individuals within it. An atmosphere is created which encourages deep contacts. Relationships between members of the group are symbolically lived through them: fairy-tales and myth can reflect responses by individuals to each other, ways of building relationships, of accepting their roles. In LPD, we often witness an important transformation in the room; a magical world is created, reflecting the nature of the group, a symbolic expression of its interior reality and those factors which bring the individuals closer together.

Fairy-tales and myths can have a stimulating effect. They are energy catalysts, bringing creativity to life, stirring our imaginations into an intense activity. The participants' psychic lives are reawakened or revived. Together with the intellect and conceptual intelligence, intuition and the emotions are also stimulated, all integral parts of the unconscious. Participants are therefore able to express all the richness of their originality with increased animation.

Fairy-tales and myth can have a protective function, the same function as the use of masks in the first week. They provide a freedom which we always find in classwork that uses deep imagination because they give us the protective cover of the imaginary world.

With fairy-tales and myth, then, we can reach new levels of expression. This may be universal because they involve recognizable human archetypes, and also because they lead to contact with the archaic beginnings of our psyche. They can also be individual since each participant perceives and experiences them according to a personal perspective and background.

The way we listen to and understand the fairy-tale or myth is not only affected by the values they communicate and by their part in our cultural heritage; we also associate them with the different stages of our psychic development, especially our childhood, and project significance on them according to our present state, including how our lives are reflected in them.

Every fairy-tale or myth carries a multiplicity of significance and it is often the latent meaning that surfaces rather than the immediate and more obvious one. Communication between participants is therefore enriched in spite of the seeming simplicity of the story. An unconscious communication provides support, enriching and giving shades of meaning to conscious verbal communication. Fairy-tales and myth speak to us but also make us speak through their evocative power. Indeed, participants often experiment with poetry in the foreign language. What results is a language full of images and colours, often loaded with connotative values.

6.2 Warm-up

6.2.1 Initial warm-up exercise

In order to stimulate participants to use their inner resources, it may be necessary for them to discover the productive use of their imagination, so helping them to make the transition to creative expression. Here are some of the techniques used in LPD; try some of them, or create new ones of your own.

Names and character

The class stands in a circle. One participant says his or her name and then adopts a pose related to the name of a fictional person or animal in a fairy-tale. The class repeats the participant's first name and adopts the same pose. Then a second participant states his or her own name, followed by the name of a fictional person or animal in a fairy-tale, and so on.

From body to character

The participants walk around the room and then, at a signal from the animator, freeze wherever they are. At each new signal—a light tap on the tambourine, a clicking noise from the fingers or tongue—

the participants change their position. After repeating this a number of times, the animator asks them to close their eyes and imagine a fictional character who is in an identical position.

When they have thought of a character, they open their eyes. At a new signal they start to move, imagining their chosen character and moving in an appropriate way. They come across other participants but do not say who they are. It is not a matter of saying 'I'm Bluebeard. Who are you?' but of coming directly into contact with others as Bluebeard.

The Tower of Babel

In biblical mythology we find two stories about language. One is the Tower of Babel, the myth of the birth of language, in which language is presented as an instrument of separation and differentiation. The other myth is the Gift of Tongues given to the Apostles after the Pentecost, in which speech has a unifying effect. We have not so far thought of an exercise to base on the second myth but the Tower of Babel offers a useful introduction to the world of myths, as explained below.

Participants enact the Tower of Babel situation while walking around the room; they express themselves not with words but with grunts and mumbles. Dialogues can take place in this way. A variation in a class which includes people of more than one linguistic background, is to suggest that they express themselves in their first languages.

This exercise tends to liberate expression; it prepares the way for an uninhibited and playful use of language.

The multiple character

Everyone in the class plays the same character in a well-known fairy-tale, Snow White, for instance. During a relaxation period, each participant imagines what moment in the fairy-tale matters most for them, what the character might say and do. They then move around the room repeating the same phrase and action several times. After a while, they can begin to extend their character and the story-line by expressing themselves more freely.[1]

1 This exercise was created by a class in an LPD programme as a consequence of two participants imagining they were Little Red Riding Hood.

6.2.2   From warm-up to performance

These warm-up exercises lead on directly to a performance.

Sentence by sentence

This warm-up exercise is taken from psychodrama, where the story is sometimes used for its symbolic function, with a view to individualized work. One participant says a sentence which represents the beginning of a story, his or her neighbour says the second, and so on. Once a story has been created in this way, the roles are allocated and performed.

The first sentence

The class is divided into groups; each is given an opening sentence as in the previous exercise, e.g. 'Once there was someone who was a little strange ...'. The number of people who will perform corresponds to the number in each group. The groups then have fifteen minutes to complete their stories. (A written activity could be suggested at this point, though we have only used it orally.) The roles are then allotted to the members of another group who perform the story-line.

The developing character

The participants are asked to close their eyes, relax, and feel comfortable, concentrate on themselves, their body position, and whatever sensations they are experiencing. The animator asks them to imagine a fictional character or creature who is some distance away. The character gradually comes nearer, stopping at the distance they want. They can see it close to and observe its behaviour. The character speaks one statement. Then the character becomes transparent and each participant becomes the character and they all stand up. The participants then make contact with others and repeat variations on this one statement. Little by little, they are led into making longer statements as a dialogue develops out of the key sentence. This technique, used on the eleventh day of an intensive course by beginners and false beginners, once resulted in meetings which focused on two Little Red Riding Hoods. The class divided into two groups, one behind each Little Red Riding Hood, supporting each protagonist. A meeting between the two Little Red Riding Hoods took place. This led us to discover that the two Little Red Riding Hoods had different grandmothers—one living in the north of the forest, the other in the south.

In the afternoon, the class divided into two groups of journalists. Each group, supported by an animator, prepared a short report on one event which has taken place during the morning's activity, an interview, and a short advert for a character from the other group. In one session, Sleeping Beauty, who had not found her husband in the morning, was the subject of one such advert.

Each group prepared an interview with a character from the other group. The subject of one interview was a unicorn; it carried on its back a young girl who wanted to cross a river. A participant had invented this story, and developed his character during the morning in response to the questions of the group in the interview. Since it did not belong to the panoply of traditional stories, the class found the character full of mystery and wanted to ask many more questions.

Using these techniques, three types of simple text are produced: one tells the story, one takes the form of a small advertisement, the third is an interview. The animators act as a language resource when the groups are not able to find the right words or structures.

Other types of written work become possible. The participants could imagine themselves in the role of a character and write about what happened—a letter from Little Red Riding Hood to her paternal grandmother, for example. Perhaps they could write to another character, such as a fish in the river writing to the unicorn.

We recommend written pieces created in groups at this point as a means of making positive use of the participants' different levels of ability. This way of working encourages a co-operative attitude and avoids leaving the animator the only source of language information.

6.3   Dramatization

Let us now examine two techniques for performing fairy-tales or myth. We have used them many times, and variations on them are suggested. We will begin with a particular tale, Little Red Riding Hood, and various techniques will be presented which gradually give rise to a world of stories through puppet-making. Finally, a technique is described which helps in creating new story-lines.

Little Red Riding Hood

One day, when we were visiting the Maeght Foundation Museum in Saint-Paul-de-Vence, my wife showed me a little book illustrated by Warja Lavater, *Le Petit Chaperon Rouge* (*Little Red Riding Hood* 1965), using a technique involving different coloured washes. I was immediately attracted by the idea of using the same technique in teaching and used it with beginners and false beginners in French who had completed a two-week LPD course, i.e. sixty hours of

French. It has also been used by various groups of LPD animators on the fourth weekend of a course.

Presenting the story

After one of the warm-ups described above which sensitizes the participants to the world of fairy-tales, we begin the session by opening the book at page 3, without identifying the story. Page 3 shows a forest symbolized by different shades of green inks. The mother's house is a large brown rectangle, the mother a patch of yellow, and Little Red Riding Hood is a small red dot.

We ask participants to interpret this picture, gently encouraging them to interpret the uses of colour, shapes, etc. so that the story is gradually identified. It usually takes until page 6 or 7 before participants discover that the story is Little Red Riding Hood. We then show them the title, after which we continue with the story. Participants make comments and the animators provide language support as required.

Choosing the main scenes

Next, we display the book, which is in the form of a folder, opening it out entirely. We then give each participant three small stickers in different colours (the sort used in offices) and ask them to choose three illustrations in the book which they think are especially

significant. They mark their choices putting their stickers on three scenes. Participants then remove stickers from scenes with the fewest stickers and move them to scenes which have more stickers. This process is repeated until the class has selected the three main scenes to use. In this way, the group can concentrate on the scenes they relate to most strongly. Having used this technique on several occasions we can confirm that the scenes chosen vary from one class to another.

Choosing the characters

We now suggest taking the first scene they have chosen and assigning roles for a performance. At this point, depending on the class, various approaches can be adopted:

Participants can be asked to volunteer and choose their own roles or the class as a whole decides which participants should take which roles. In this case, the participants only accept if they are happy to be chosen. Sometimes, several people are chosen for the same part, and if this happens, each of the three scenes can be played in different ways with a different cast. This varies the content and reinforces the acquisition of the language.

If the class is responsive, we ask the participants to give reasons for their choices: 'I would like so-and-so to play that part because ...', but we take care at this point to avoid any inappropriate reasoning. It is worth noting that the expression of personal opinion 'I think/believe that ...' occurs here very frequently.

Putting on a scene

Once the roles for the first scene have been agreed, it can be performed. It is advisable to concentrate the action on the encounter between just two characters. To do this, use the techniques described in Chapter 5, involving sequence variations with the use of double and role-reversal techniques pages 113–14, 119.

By way of illustration, here is an example of what happened in one class. After a farewell scene between Little Red Riding Hood and her mother, one participant, acting as the protagonist, chose the role of a tree in the forest, witnessing the meeting between Little Red Riding Hood and the Wolf. She performed the role of commentator, or chorus, as in classical Greek drama. She stood with her arms outstretched to represent branches and accompanied her verbal expression with a balancing movement, like a tree bending in the wind.

The animator, acting as double, took up the same position behind her and reproduced, as closely as possible, her movements, rhythm, and tone of voice. She was ready to give any language help needed,

although there were not many corrections. The rest of the class,
standing in different parts of the room, represented other forest
trees, copying the body, voice and verbal expressions of the protagonist in mirror and echo. The members of the class echoed the animator's support when the protagonist made mistakes.

The protagonist had had only one year of French in school, five
years earlier. The activity took place on day nine, some 43 hours into
an intensive course.

The text of this activity was taped and transcribed in full. Here is
the beginning of it:

P = Protagonist
C = members of the class who repeat in chorus
A = animator

P   I am a tree! (c) I am a tree! (c) I am old. (c) I am a granddaddy.
     (correction offered by A: 'a grandfather')
P   I am a grandfather. (c)
P   But, what's happening? (c) Oh, I don't want to see anything. (c)
     (alteration offered by A: 'I can't see anything')
P   I can't see anything. (c)
P   I can't see anything. (c) Oh! The little child. (c) What is she
     doing? (c) She's picking flowers. (c) Little flowers. (c) That's
     strange! (c) A handsome child. (correction offered by A: 'a beau-
     tiful child')
P   A beautiful child. (c)
P   I like children go for walk.
     (correction offered by A: '... who go for walks')
P   ... who go for walks. (c)
P   I like children who go for walks in the forest. (c) I am strong. (c)
     But I am also kind, especially with children. (c) Oh! Oh, Red
     Riding Hood. (c) But, Oh! I can see the Wolf. (c) Where is Little
     Red Riding Hood? (c) Oh! The Wolf and Little Red Riding
     Hood! (c) I can't see!
     (correction offered by A: 'I can't watch')
P   I can't watch! (c)
P   What is the wolf doing? (c) I am strong! (c) (watches the scene)
     The Wolf is kind to Red Riding Hood. (c) It's dangerous! (c) It's
     dangerous. It's dangerous. The Wolf is going under ... with ...
     without Little Red Riding Hood! (c) It's not possible. (c) It's the
     first time. (c) What does the Wolf want?
     (correction offered by A: 'I wonder what the Wolf wants')

While the protagonist was speaking, she did not feel isolated or suffocated by the others. The class shared in the experience, re-echoing the text. Their roles as mirrors reinforced both and stimulated her expression. And a rhythmic relationship was created between the class and protagonist through the return of the echo.

Remarks on the language used in this example:

- Language was experienced by the protagonist as a whole person and was set in a context created by the class. At this point the protagonist used linguistic knowledge she had acquired during the course. The animator's corrections, kept to a minimum, added to or refined this knowledge, a process which would be stepped up in a second phase.
- Comprehension was evident not just in terms of the words used but of expression as a whole, including attitudes, movements, tone of voice, rhythm, and melody. The technique of the class as trees mirroring the protagonist encouraged them to listen carefully and express themselves using body language and tone of voice as well as vocabulary.
- Retention was facilitated by the movements which accompanied the language, without any specific exercise or other attempt to memorize.

A later scene takes place in the grandmother's house and the tale is continued step by step. Depending on the particular scene, the participants may be protagonists, antagonists, or part of the scenery. There is no show as such, no stage, and no audience, just a performance in which the world of the imagination becomes symbolic and reflects inner reality.

The use of space during the different scenes and the varying configurations adopted by the participants are not only meaningful in relation to the central activity but reflect the life of the group and the relationships between its members.

6.4   Creating a fairy-tale

6.4.1   Sticky labels

We once proposed this technique to a group of teachers who had worked with Lavater's illustrations of Little Red Riding Hood. It can also be used with participants on a language course.

Participants divide into two groups; each group is given several connected sheets of computer paper together with some coloured stickers. The animator then asks them to make up a story following Lavater's approach, using stickers as symbols which can be torn to make different shapes and combined to make illustrations. When they have finished the illustrations, they are asked to prepare a story-line and its text. Some classes may like to write it down. Language teachers training in LPD can write the text in a language, or more than one, which is common to them or which they teach. For participants who are learners, the linguistic level of the text will, of course, be much less advanced.

When everyone has finished, the two groups meet to discover the story the other group has created. Each group explains what it has produced and presents the text in the context of the drawings. Here is a translation of the text created by a group of language teachers training in LPD:

> Once upon a time there was a little caterpillar which lived high in a tall green lime tree. Every day she had the same dream: of flying like the birds she could see from her hiding-place, a curled-up leaf. One day a large black bird landed near her leaf. It was a goshawk.

> The little caterpillar, terribly frightened, squeezed down into the bottom of the leaf, but the goshawk's piercing eyes had already discovered her and he said, 'Little caterpillar, don't be afraid, I won't eat you!' The little caterpillar came out of her hiding-place and said, 'Oh, Goshawk, if you aren't going to eat me, take me on your mighty wings and carry me to the clouds. I want to fly like a bird at least once in my life.'

The goshawk was surprised, but agreed. He had never had a friend to travel with him. Now, he would never be alone on his long flights through the sky. 'Snuggle under my feathers, then the wind won't trouble you', he said. The caterpillar did as he told her, and they took off towards the clouds. They were both happy to be together; the caterpillar could see all the things she had never seen before, and the goshawk no longer felt lonely.

The days went by and they were both happy. One day the caterpillar felt that something was happening to her. The goshawk noticed too, and said, 'What's the matter, little caterpillar? I can hardly feel you. Are you still there?' She made no reply. He perched in the nearest tree, where he could not believe his eyes. A splendid multi-coloured butterfly emerged from under his black wings and took flight. 'Thank you so much, and farewell, dear Goshawk' said the butterfly ... and disappeared. The goshawk stayed there, sitting on a branch, feeling very sad. But what happened next? He heard a little rustling in the green leaves. Another little caterpillar was emerging from its hiding-place.

One could pose questions about the symbolic meaning of this text; naive analysts might find in it a fine example of the inner metamorphosis which some of the participants experienced during the course.

6.4.2　Puppets

Participants are asked to bring two empty toilet rolls, some leftover pieces of fabric, wool, glue, scissors, pins, and a stapler. With all these

materials piled together on a tablecloth in the middle of the room, the participants are given just half an hour to make two puppets each.[2]

The reason for limiting the time for making the puppets is that participants will realize they cannot make masterpieces in such a short time. This relieves any pressure to achieve an 'artistic' design.

The animators also make two puppets. When they have finished, they join the other members of the class who have finished or are about to finish and begin short dialogues with their puppets. This phase of informal contact allows participants the opportunity to begin to define the identity of their puppets and give them psychological depth. Because the participants have made their own puppets, they already know them well, identify with them and can project their imagination into giving them personalities.

The meeting of the puppets

First meeting

Afterwards, with everyone sitting in a circle, we sometimes arrange for each puppet to be briefly introduced to others in the class. The puppets are brought together, and are asked who they would like to meet. A clown, for example, might want to chat to an old peasant woman, while the beauty queen might want to talk to the pirate ... Two participants, A and B, as protagonists, come face to face, each with a puppet, each doubled by an animator and one half of the class. They have a conversation.

The next step can be as follows. The whole class can carry out dialogues in pairs after the meeting of the first two protagonists. Each participant in group A in the role of the puppet A meets a participant in group B in the role of puppet B. After that it is possible to shift the pairs.

Shifting technique

The two protagonists (A and B) then choose two other participants (C and D) to meet and chat to. There are now two encounters taking place at the same time. Each person can, if they choose to, ask another participant to give support as double. The doubles can then take the place of the protagonists (relay technique). Finally, if it seems useful, there can be a meeting between the original two protagonists but this time without support from other participants or from the animators, unless one of them runs into particular difficulty.

Extension

There are several ways to develop these encounters: Each of the four participants above (A, B, C, D) meets another participant so that four encounters are now taking place, directly involving eight participants in a dialogue (step 3). All the other members of the class double. It may be possible to extend the meeting of the four participants in a next step (step 4), with two interlocutors at the same time (subgroups of three persons) so that twelve participants become directly involved in the meeting.

This allows for a new development of the sequence around the 'core' of the meeting of the first two protagonists.

When participants have expressed themselves with their own puppets, they can share each other's puppets so that they can work with unfamiliar puppets, which gives rise to interesting projections and new language practice.

6.4.3   String stories

Another possible technique relates to a form of African story-telling. In some oral traditions, the story-teller shows a necklace or thread on to which are attached tokens which identify the tales in their repertoire. Members of the audience choose one and, in return for a suitable payment, listen to the story. This technique can be used in the classroom.

Cut string into different lengths, make knots in some, put a paper clip on one, two buttons on another, and so on, so that there is a choice of 'tokens'. Here is one example of how this technique has been used: after telling participants the origin of this idea, they are told a French joke, using a length of thread with a large knot at one end and a smaller knot at the other which are kept hidden in the left hand at first. The animator has already prepared more lengths of knotted string to use later. The animator then tells a story.

> Once upon a time there was a little earthworm, just born, who came out of the earth for the first time on a lovely Spring day.

(At this point, the end of string with the large knot is revealed between the middle and index fingers of the left hand.)

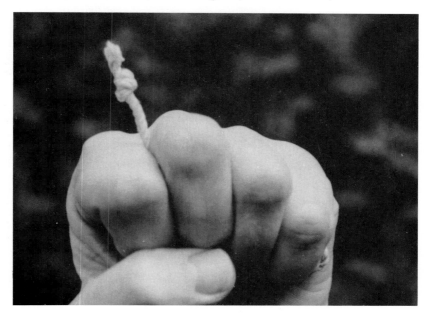

> The little worm stretches, looks round and says: 'Oh, what a nice day, the light is so lovely! The flowers smell so good, such scent, such colours! Nature is so lovely!'
>
> Suddenly, something moves near him and starts to come out of the ground.

(At this point, the other end of the string with the smaller knot is revealed between the ring finger and little finger on the left hand.)

> The little worm hears a grumpy voice saying, 'Oh, it's so cold, it's horrible. Ugh! Not me, I don't want to go out.' He turns towards the newcomer and says, 'What? Can't you smell the scent of the flowers?' 'No!' 'Can't you see how beautiful nature is?' 'No!' the

newcomer answers, in a sulky voice. 'But how can that be?' asks
the earthworm. And the other voice replies crossly, 'Because I'm
your tail!'

The participants are then asked to divide into groups of three or four,
the lengths of knotted string are placed on a chair, and they are invited to take one and make up their own story. The result on one
course was five stories, of which the following is an example:

> Once upon a time there was a little horse which was different from
> all the others—it could only gallop in circles.

(The story-teller had bent one of the strings in this right hand to
suggest the shape of a horse. When the horse had to go in a circle, he
held the other end of the string in his left hand and moved his right
hand round his left.)

> The other horses laughed at him, and it made him very unhappy.
> One day, when he couldn't stand the jeers any more he ran away as
> far as he could go. Towards the end of the afternoon, he came to a
> big round tent and began to eat the grass, still crying hot tears.

> At this moment a man with a fat stomach left the tent and saw
> him. He said, 'Why are you crying?' The horse explained that other
> horses made fun of him because he always ran in circles. The man
> said, 'But you're just the sort of horse I'm looking for! I'm the
> circus master, and you can run in circles as much as you like.'

> That very evening the little horse started his new job. He ran
> round the circus ring several times, amusing the audience with

tricks, neighing with pleasure at their applause, rearing up on his hind legs to show how happy he felt. He was a huge success. The little horse had never been so happy.

6.5 Using myth

The warm-up techniques are used as for the fairy-tales but this time with a deliberate focus on a mythical being. From experience it does not seem necessary to develop any techniques different from those described for fairy-tales. Here is one example of how myths have been exploited during an LPD course.

A Bible was brought into the room. Using religious subjects is open to debate but we overcame our doubts and did the following activity:

Following the standard relaxation period and warm-up exercises, we spoke to the class about this new exercise and about our reservations. The class did not share them, so we took the Bible, ostentatiously putting it upside down, and told them what we could remember of the chosen biblical myth, the story of Adam, Eve, and the Serpent.

We expected a meeting of the Serpent with Adam and Eve—a triadic meeting. However, group dynamics led us in another direction. The dialogue between the Serpent and Eve was so productive and so charged with meaning that Adam had no opportunity to express himself at all that morning! Here is one example.

The class divided into two, one half taking the part of the Serpent and the other that of Eve. The two animators went from one to the other giving them linguistic support.

After that the animators sat in the centre as protagonists, each with a group as doubles: the animators' function was to repeat what their doubles gave, making corrections to the language as necessary but adding nothing new. This particular arrangement did not work out because there were times when the animators simply could not keep up with everything that was being said. Participants could not wait for the animators to hear what one person had to say before saying what *they* wanted to say, others spoke directly to the opposite group or individual members of that group. But the linguistic energy in the class was very high!

This myth had touched on topics that were important for the groups, which explains why the language was expressed and projected so readily. Afterwards, several participants remarked that they had not even realized they were expressing themselves in the foreign language!

Each time a myth that has a similar strong meaning has been used we have experienced the same tremendous energy of expression. At times, participants suddenly become aware of consciousness-raising related to the symbolic sense of what is happening. I recall one woman participant on a course who had chosen a dragon as her mythical figure, saying to the class, in a way that suggested a flash of personal intuition, 'It's no accident that the dragon has come into my mind'.

One difficulty is to choose an appropriate myth, to enter into its world oneself in order to relate oneself to the issues it raises, and then to find the most appropriate way of approaching the group's dynamic. In our view, myth must be dealt with more delicately than fairy-tales, because of the force of its impact. It might be prudent not to engage in myth unless one has experienced the full effect personally first, and so to be in a position to understand the experience from the point of view of a participant.

6.6   Conclusion

Through the exercises we have developed in this chapter we are exploring the symbolic aspects of human expression. These allow the unconscious to express itself in a more direct way and strongly stimulate participants' imagination and feelings.

Other means of expression in this symbolic domain are open to us. For instance, we are now using Chinese ideograms, letters of the Hebrew alphabet, geometrical figures (e.g. an encounter between a square and a circle), and Tarot cards as a means not of telling the future, but of projecting the world of the imagination (e.g. a meeting between the characters of two different cards). There are many other ways.

When we use these procedures in an intensive course, we do not finish at this level, but we prepare participants to join the more prosaic outside with exercises we have presented in the previous chapter (5.6). In this way, participants can leave the course with their heads in the clouds and their feet on the ground.

7 Written expression

Writing is a painting of the voice. [V O L T A I R E]

7.1 Techniques for approaching written expression in LPD

We shall begin by describing some of the wide range of possible written activities.

7.1.1 Sensitizing to intonation through writing

In Chapter 4, we examined the importance given in LPD to the perception of the rhythmic and intonational components of the foreign language, and thereafter to the perception of the connotative values of the message. Here are three examples to illustrate how some of these elements can be represented in spatial terms.

Vocalizing a written pronoun

Participants are asked to write the pronoun 'I' in the target language on the reverse of a blank sheet of paper. They can choose any shape,

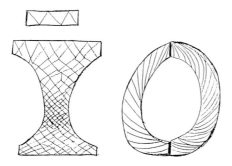

Example by an Italian participant

size, or position. When they have identified a design they are happy
with, they are asked to reproduce it on the front of the paper, in the
size and place they prefer. A small, ornate 'I' in the corner of the page
does not have the same effect as a large, stark 'I' in the middle. Each
participant then shows his or her 'I' and pronounces it in a way they
feel suits the way in which they have drawn it. The word is repeated
in echo by the class.

Visual poetry

Visual poetry can be used to help participants see how the same
thing can be said in many different ways, and to sensitize them to
changes in the meaning of words according to how they are
expressed. The warm-up exercises for the activity uses M. Leiris's *Le
Cercle Miroitant* (*The Glittering Circle*) or my poem below:

```
        B
          o
            n
              h
            C o e u r
            o  a
            r    l
            p        m
            s          e
```

Participants divide into groups of two or three in order to find
different ways of reading this poem. The graphic presentation of the
poem encourages the discovery of a range of tonal interpretations
which are then shared with the class as a whole. Participants are next
asked to close their eyes and think of one of their favourite words in
the foreign language. They may like the word because of its sound or
its associations. They are asked to open their eyes when they have
identified their word. They are then asked to represent their word
graphically, as in the following example by a participant in a French
class:

```
     s O L E I L
     L E V A N T
```

When the drawings are finished, participants form small groups to draw a picture which combines different words, as in the following example:

```
          I         L
       O L E I
     S           L
  A     LEVANT
  M         O
  O       O
  U         U
  R           E
              T
                T
                  E
```

The participants then prepare a reading of their poem.

A favourite word

In this approach, participants are invited to choose any word in the target language which they particularly like, for example, *love, sun, music, energy, money, you, jumping*. Encourage them to select a word with no more than seven letters. If they are not sure about the spelling, ask them to make a guess and then tell them whether the guess is right or wrong until they arrive at the correct spelling. It may be necessary in some cases to spell the word for them. The class then forms pairs with one person, participant A, sitting opposite the other, participant B. Participant A brings one arm forward in front of B and draws his or her word in the air with a pointed finger so that B can 'read' it. B then raises an arm and, using a pointed finger, joins with A to write the word in the air. When the partners are in harmony, B says A's word and A confirms whether B is right or wrong.

A can then change the style of writing the word (bigger or smaller letters, using block capitals, changing the writing rhythm, emphasizing one part of the spelling, etc.) while B tries saying the word according to these various changes, for example, quietly and carefully to match small, deliberate writing, or fast and firmly to match a similar rhythm of A's writing.

The roles in each pair are then reversed with B writing his or her chosen word for A to copy.

Afterwards, the class comes together in a circle. Each member presents a word three times, first writing it in the air in silence, then saying the word out loud, and finally with the class writing the word in the air and saying it in echo.

In a final stage, participants can form groups of three or four, with each participant expressing a particular form and rhythm for their chosen word in writing on a sheet of paper. The words are then presented to the whole class in the form of the written text which other members can read aloud. The participant who had chosen the word then says whether the style of expressing the word in speech is that which he or she had tried to describe in writing.

These exercises help participants to experience writing as an act of personal expression. The word is brought to life in its new graphical form and its connotative components are discovered in its visual resonance.

7.1.2   Creating poems

We identified in *Rhythms and poems* (Chapter 4) the importance given to poetry in sensitizing participants to the rhythmic and melodic characteristics of the target language, not just to the connotative values of the message. At first sight, it would seem too ambitious to want to ask participants to compose poems in a foreign language. But, with clear directions and in a supportive environment, productivity can be greatly increased. Learners derive great satisfaction from creating poetry.

In Chapter 4, we also saw how to create poems in particular rhythms (4.2.2). Here are some further examples:

Participle poem

It is possible to ask participants to compose poems using particular categories, for example, participles. The use of present participles offers fairly easy rhythmic creations because of the strong influence of the sound *-ing* (e.g. *starting, going, learning, running*). Here is the beginning of a poem using past participles in French:

	Translation
Sorti	Went out
Parti	Left
Enfui	Ran away
Fini ...	Finished ...

Essential grammatical correction by the animator of a poetic text produced by a participant can be followed by an exercise to bring out its rhythm and melody. Perhaps the animator can read a published or known poem to the class, for example, Jean Tardieu's *Participes* to a class learning French. These poems demonstrate that published poetry is created using exactly the same approach, which helps to confirm to the participants the value of their work.

Grammatical poem

Participants working in small groups construct a set of phrases beginning with a chosen word, for example, 'If ..', 'When ...' or 'Yes'. A variation consists of creating verses of just two lines, the first beginning with one chosen word, the second with another, for example, 'When ...' and 'Then ...'. Here is an example in which the writer must use 'If ...' and 'I ...' and also has to repeat the first part: 'If I had money, I ...'. Actual examples in French from an LPD session are:

	Translation
Si j'avais de l'argent,	If I had money,
Je serais très content.	I would be very happy.
Si j'avais de l'argent,	If I had money,
J'aurais beaucoup de temps.	I would have plenty of time.
Si j'avais de l'argent,	If I had money,
Je quitterais mon amant.	I would leave my lover.

It is obvious that such an exercise helps to practise a particular structure or set of vocabulary. In the example above, the use of the conditional is practised.

Advice

Participants work in small groups and create a text made up of orders or advice given to them, or overheard when they were children:

Behave yourself.
Finish your soup.
Say hello to the lady.

The accumulation of short sentences which use imperatives gives a precise rhythm to the text, thus offering many opportunities to practise intonation as well as giving the participants' text an immediately identifiable poetic quality.

The X poem

This poem has a simple construction, X, with four words joined by the conjunction 'and', for example:

Complementarity

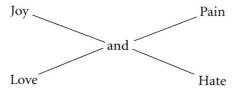

Joy   Pain

and

Love   Hate

Using an example like this one, participants are divided into small groups of four and each member can contribute one word to the X. The group can then agree a suitable title. In some cases, participants may decide on the title and then choose the vocabulary. Participants in their groups can explore a variety of ways to recite their poem including a variety of changes in voice.

A poem can be created using vocabulary with a suffix or prefix in common. As in the example above, it can be written down with a design which demonstrates the link between the words. Here is an example using the suffix -*tion*:

```
              E T
       E   M   N
     M O  A T N          T
    O  A                 I
 -TION ... CONFRONTA-    O
      S A A C            N
   E N   C I
 S       L P
     S     M
           O C
```

More advanced participants can form small groups and try to create similar poetic displays. They can then practise reading their poems aloud to other members of the class.

7.1.3   Experience and imagination as sources for writing

Written activities stemming from experience production within a class have been described in Chapters 5 and 6. Material is generated by the personal qualities of the class, and so varies according to the participants involved; different kinds of text appear—reports, letters between characters, stories, and so on, as well as an infinite variety of themes and situations.

In LPD, using the actual imagination of the individuals in a class is our preferred means of leading participants towards a confident use of written expression. I have, for example, sometimes asked classes to produce material on the theme of *prison* after having asked them to make a picture connected to the word 'prison' and having done oral activities using the picture.[1]

We owe this idea to Mario Rinvolucri, and have used it in different groups and in different forms (Dufeu 1993).

Here are several different kinds of text produced by participants in response to the topics they themselves suggested:

- Taking notes from the prisoner or a member of his or her family after a discussion with the lawyer, or the lawyer's notes during or after the interview with a client.
- A newspaper advertisement asking for a pen-pal outside the jail.
- Secret messages between prisoners preparing to escape.
- A letter to a boyfriend, girlfriend, relative, friend, etc.
- A letter to the prison governor complaining about jail conditions.
- A proposal for a prison regime drawn up by prisoners.
- A newspaper article reporting an escape, an interview with a prisoner, or a case of injustice.
- A speech by the defence lawyer.

7.1.4 Written text and oral production

It is popular and very productive to organize simple dramatizations of written texts. In LPD, texts are selected according to two basic criteria:

Relational

We choose written materials which engage participants either directly or symbolically and with which they can therefore either identify or react.

Dramaturgic

We choose written texts which lend themselves to LPD objectives as outlined in Chapter 1 (1.4.1 and 1.5.2). Here are some examples:

A young girl loves a young man, who loves her. The parents on both sides agree with the marriage. It is a beautiful story, but on the dramaturgical level nothing happens. However, if the father wants his daughter not to marry the young man, but an old disagreeable rich neighbour, we get not only a play by Molière but the expression of opposed dramaturgical forces. We have a wish (the union of both young people), opposition (against the father's and the old rich man's wishes) and we can possibly have the support of other people on each side.

These dramaturgic forces 'wish' and 'opposition' are not only in plays, but also in literary texts, in newspaper articles, in politics, etc. They can be found in everyday situations. The participants are then stimulated to express their position, and this gives rise to a need for language which can be fulfilled by the trainers and the other participants.

Using these criteria I have, for example, used stories and myths (Chapter 6), metaphors, extracts from Saint-Exupéry's *Le petit prince* (*The Little Prince*), and La Fontaine's fables. More advanced participants find passages from emotive texts such as Anouilh's *Antigone*, Keats' *Eve of St Agnes*, or Gide's *Return of the Prodigal Son* particularly stimulating.

Dramatization often awakens curiosity in the books from which the texts are taken. Some participants, for example, bought *The Little Prince* after the LPD course ended. They read all the passages we had selected, and then the book as a whole.

One exercise consisting of dramatizing newspaper texts, in the tradition of Moreno's *Living Newspaper* and Boal's *Newspaper Theatre*, has been described on numerous occasions by Daniel Feldhendler, with whom we have worked in developing relational dramaturgy (Feldhendler 1988, 1989, 1990).

7.1.5   From written text to written production

Here are some examples of activities to illustrate how an LPD class extends from a written script to their own creative writing. In the first example, the class has heard the text about a man leaving a woman early in the morning (Prévert: *Déjeuner du matin*).

The class divides into two groups which face each other some distance apart. One group represents 'the man' who leaves, the other, 'the woman' he has abandoned. Different attitudes or poses are taken in turn by a participant from each group: a 'man' comes to the centre and assumes an attitude which corresponds to how he interprets the character he is portraying; a 'woman' comes forward to respond to him by adopting a contrasting attitude, the 'man' withdraws, leaving an empty space. The woman stays in her position, waiting for another 'man' to take up another attitude opposite her, then returns to her group, when her place is taken by another representative of that group, and so on. When this exercise has been thoroughly understood, short dialogues between each new couple become possible, beginning with interjections and gradually working up to longer exchanges. Written messages can then be exchanged between the two groups, maintaining the same personalities.

Sometimes, we extend the exercise by reversing the roles of the groups, with the 'man' taking the part of the 'woman'. This enables participants to consider the situation from opposite perspectives and often leads to a change of style in how the characters are portrayed. In dramatic terms, such exercises reveal the association of different forces represented by the two characters, supported by the various attitudes taken by the participants. In terms of relations, the topic engages the interest of those taking part because it concerns parting, saying goodbye, or separation, in other words, themes with which we can all identify. Linguistically, the participants are confronted with specific lexical and structural items in formulating letters or messages between the two protagonists.

In another activity, the class is again divided into two groups which will alternatively represent two characters. Both groups are asked to write a letter which reflects the personality, interests, experiences, etc. of the first character. This letter is meant for the other group, who, after receiving the first letter, replies in the character of the second person. In the situation described above, both groups might first prepare a letter in the role of the 'woman'. They would then exchange their messages and in a second phase, they would reply in the role of the 'man'.

7.1.6 From text to dramatization; from dramatization to text

It is also possible for a class to stage a scene which has been created by all the participants, starting without any previous rehearsal, for instance, with a tableau vivant. This is subsequently written down as a script, and presented a second time. In this way, there are alternating oral and written phases.[2]

2 This approach recalls some of Vladimir N. Iljine's principles of therapeutic theatre (Petzold 1982).

The lure of the vacuum

Texts which contain blanks are often used for control tests. They can also be used creatively, as in the following variations: we have used, for example, a passage from a newspaper which relates the story of a man waiting impatiently for his wife to return to him. We omitted the final sentence. We asked the class to divide into groups of three, and to try to provide the missing line. They could consider when? how? why? whether? etc. After sharing their responses as a class, the participants wanted to know how the original story ended. They were surprised to learn that it was 'Then she will be able to do the washing-up'.

Many written activities could have been developed from this basic text, including letters from the woman to her husband while she was away, notes telling him what to do while she is away, and letters to the Women's Liberation Movement.

In the café

This example of an activity used a poem by the Algerian poet Rachid Boudfedra in which he describes himself sitting comfortably on the terrace of a café, reading the paper and drinking a glass of wine. The poem ends with the words 'And I asked myself if I was a revolutionary'. We blanked out the last word and gave copies to participants (beginners with only 50 hours of French) without any explanation. We asked them to write on the board any word which came to mind as a result of reading the poem. This approach meant that the participants read the poem several times, and familiarized themselves with it. We gave equivalents in French if they did not know or understand the words. Then we underlined the words on the board which came closest to the omitted word. This helped them to find the right word.

Night visit

At other times we have used a psychological test to stimulate discussion. Here is how it starts:

Imagine you are going for a walk. What time of year is it?

Each participant gives the name of the season he or she has in mind. Then we ask:

What time of day is it? ... You are entering a forest. What is the path like? etc.

We have transposed this principle into a written form. Participants take a sheet of paper and complete the following:

It is eleven o'clock at night. The moon is hidden behind the clouds, a heavy silence accompanies the steps of a man who stops in front of a large house. His silhouette is seen by the light of a lamp. (Describe this man.) He stays in front of the front door for a moment, then, after opening it with much difficulty, goes into the hall, where a green lamp is shining on a strange object. (Describe this object.)

Slowly, without making any noise, he goes into the sitting room. A woman is asleep in an old armchair. (Describe the woman.) She is dreaming. (What is she dreaming about?) When the man is just a few steps away she wakes up. She looks at him in astonishment and says: (What does she say?) The man's face is transformed

when he hears her, and a strange idea comes into his mind.
(Complete the story.)

The texts are extended by participants in small groups before being read to the class as a whole. Animators who use this exercise could take topics from their course material.

Peripheral vision

Concentration on a task to be completed can, at the same time, help familiarize participants with linguistic phenomena, a principle illustrated in the following example which is an extract from an introduction to a book:

> I think that **imagination** is stronger than **science**, that **myth** is more convincing than **history**; that **dreams** are more powerful than **facts**; that **hope** has always triumphed over **experience**; that **life** is the only remedy for **worry**. And I believe that **love** is stronger than **death**. (Fulghum)

We blanked out the words in bold and asked the participants, again in small groups, to complete the text. While they were doing it, they were getting to know some comparative forms in the target language.

Sub-editing

The participants, in groups of four, are given a letter. They must make cuts so that it contains a minimum number of words for sending as a telegram; but it must contain all the essential details of the message. The group then share their solutions with each other.

Padding

This activity shares the same principle as the previous one but in reverse. Beginning with a key word written on a large piece of paper, for example, *holidays, adventure, future, forbidden, solitude, injustice,* participants write down their private associations with some or all of the words. They then form small groups to choose from the associations offered and write a short story or message.

7.2 Developing written expression in different types of text

We shall now consider possible creative activities using different types of texts written by participants.

7.2.1 Letters

Writing a letter can, of course, stimulate the imagination. A protest letter to Father Christmas because he is not doing his job well will use certain structures that could be useful in a letter of complaint to a business or organization. The participant can therefore choose any situation to write complaints, congratulations, invitations, requests, information, etc. It is not necessary for the animators to dictate the solution. It is even possible to send a letter to oneself, for example, containing wishes for the New Year. Here, too, the vocabulary and structures can be given a more personal and at times humorous touch. Here are two examples:

A job application

The animator asks the participants, while they are relaxing, to imagine the job they would most like to have, and to find three qualities which would be needed to make a success of that job. They then have to imagine that they see a suitable vacancy advertised in a newspaper. They write a letter of application arguing that they have the three key qualities.

The letter-writer

In many countries there are public letter-writers. Participants work in pairs. Participant A indicates to B what he or she wants to write to someone else in the class, who we will call C. B tells A what he or she wants to write to another person in the class, who we will call D. B writes A's letter to C. A writes B's letter to D. A and B write at the same time. B shows A the text and A either agrees or asks for changes before signing it. A shows B the text and B either agrees or asks for changes before signing it. A then takes the letter he or she wrote to D and B takes the other letter to C. The animator can offer information and advice to the participants while they are preparing their letters.[3]

3 We owe this idea to Mario Rinvolucri.

7.2.2 Newspapers

Some of the techniques used in LPD are known in the wider teaching world, for example, taking the title of an article and asking students to compose the text, or providing the text and asking them to give it a title. In the former case, it is possible to provide an emotive and highly descriptive title, such as 'He doesn't want to!', 'Too late!', or 'Her dream comes true!'. The sensationalist press provides us with many such examples. Titles of this kind provide endless opportunities for participants, in small groups, to create stories.

The newspaper headline

There is an activity used in LPD which illustrates the creative use of newspaper articles and headlines. Each participant has two sheets of paper and a pen or pencil. An animator asks the class to close their eyes, and gives the following instructions:

> You dream that you are getting up. You go to collect your newspaper at the front door, before having your breakfast, and on the front page you see a headline that astonishes you. Now open your eyes. Write down the headline in large print on one sheet of your paper. Now write a short article on the other sheet.

The participants then divide into groups of three. Each person passes on his or her headline to the neighbour on the right, and writes a short article to go with the headline he or she has been given. After the second exchange of headlines, a third article is written. The articles are then read in the group and other group members or the animator can suggest corrections. The final articles are then shared with the whole class.

One variation on this exercise consists of asking the class to choose one of the headlines suggested by individual participants. The participants divide into groups who write an article to go with the chosen headline. Again, these articles are shared with the whole class.

Advertisement

Make up a page of advertisements photocopied from a magazine leaving space for a new advertisement. Working in groups, participants have to write this new advertisement. The real advertisements from the magazine will give them the linguistic material and formal aspects needed for this type of text; it may be for finding or selling a house or flat, meeting someone with a view to marriage, or spending holidays or leisure time together.

Creating and replying to mysterious or amusing advertisements also stimulates written production. For example:

Flat for rent. Nightbirds preferred.
Maid of all work seeks good-for-nothing.

Publicity

Publicity leaflets offer scope for exercises, for example, where a text has to be written to match an illustration. For instance, we have asked participants at the beginning of a course in written expression to compose a text to publicize that course. They have the right, as in most advertising material, to exaggerate a little. After allowing for these exaggerations, this technique has provided us with information on what students expect from the course and above all, right from the start, helps to create a lighthearted atmosphere in the group.

Exchanging notes and changing register

It is possible to develop techniques which permit the passage from one register to another. Professional life gives us many illustrations; for example, informal notes made before or after a business call, or for a meeting, or a report, or following an interview. Here is an exercise for advanced students to help in changing register.

The three words

Phase A. Each participant in the class thinks of a situation which he or she has directly experienced or witnessed, and writes down three key words which characterize this situation on a sheet of paper.

Phase B. The papers are collected and redistributed. Each participant must now write a short story suggested from the three key words on the paper given.

Phase C. The texts are again collected and redistributed. Each participant reads the text given silently.

Phase D. Participants form pairs. A tells B the story A has read and B tells the story he or she has read.

Phase E. The class comes together again and each participant tells the others the story he or she was told.

It is interesting for the groups to go back for one or two stories, that is, to go back to Phase A and ask the authors of the three words to tell the story of what had actually happened to him or her.

7.3   Conclusion

There are many possibilities for creative uses of written expression. Those you have just read may encourage you to create others. What is crucially important in LPD is for participants to be the authors of their own text and for support texts to include subject-matter which will be of interest to them. Language is then meaningful to the individual because it has found life from within. After this important phase learners can continue their linguistic journey along their own road, in the business, technical, literary, social, political, or scientific landscape of their chosen interest or career.

PART THREE

Teacher training

8 I teach what I am

This chapter begins with a brief overview of the development of teacher training in relation to the development of linguistic methodology. The four stages in the training of language teachers are then presented, and the nature of relational training is defined more precisely. After considering some of the myths which influence the teachers' pedagogic activity, there follows a description of the training undertaken by LPD animators.

8.1 Historical overview of teacher training

One day, someone asked Picasso how long he had taken to complete a painting. He replied 'Seventy years—and twenty minutes!'

Developments in teacher training relate to the development of teaching itself as described in Chapter 1 (1.1). Anyone teaching classical languages was expected to have not only a mastery of the language taught but also a good knowledge of its grammar and, ideally, some translation techniques. In other words, a teacher had to have some intellectual understanding and to be, above all, a philologist.

The Direct Method marked the beginning of a pragmatic era in teaching, when it was no longer enough for the teacher to have an intellectual understanding of the foreign language and knowledge of the culture. He or she had, in addition, to be able to *use* the language in conversation. It is at this point that the obligatory four stages of language courses appear: revision/checking of acquisition of previous work; introduction of new linguistic material; practice work on this through sets of question and response; exercises in re-using and transferring the material to new contexts (the latter often modest or even non-existent). Then the teacher had to acquire techniques for transmitting his or her intellectual knowledge of the language, and to be able to use the language. This tendency has gradually been reinforced as pragmatic teaching has developed.

Theoretical linguistics acquired an elevated status and the language teacher was confronted by this new science, especially through structuralism. Some teachers even went as far as to flirt with Chomsky's deep structures, though without understanding exactly how this knowledge could be transposed into their courses. In some countries, attempts were made to turn teachers into linguists. Theoretical linguistics, however, was becoming increasingly autonomous, losing its way in its own labyrinths. Because some basic theoretical linguistic research took place far from the preoccupations of practising teachers, they felt increasingly ignored or abandoned, and got on with their work with less and less reference to linguistics. It is also true, however, that many British applied linguists, such as Pit Corder and Henry Widdowson, have always remained in touch with classroom concerns.[1]

At the same time, behaviourist psychology had been co-opted by structuralists so that language teaching gradually became trapped in a net of interrelated intellectual disciplines. Unfortunately, in many instances the result was an over-simplified, and at times, over-mechanistic view of learning and the learner. The association of structuralism and behaviourism led to the development of audio-aural and audio-visual methods. Increasingly, the teacher became a mere technician.

The advent of communicative teaching put even more pressure on teachers, who were now expected to devise their own strategies and modes of communication. New theoretical, practical, and personal demands sprang up. What is more, some of the results of communicative techniques turned out to be very disappointing where appropriate attitudes had not been carefully taught in advance. Changing the way we do things implies a change in the way we are; we cannot change the way we work without accepting the risk of changing ourselves. When teachers and students no longer have a set book or syllabus to refer to, their relationship becomes much more direct, so that personal training becomes indispensable.

The current concept of teacher training rewards trainees with a diploma. They then join the ranks of the seasoned professionals, holders of a professional passport for life. By contrast, LPD, as part of the Teacher Development movement, proposes a process of continuous education, in which the development of teachers continues throughout their career, involving their personal as well as their professional evolution. Let us examine this process more closely.[2]

1 See Howatt (1984: Part Four), and Widdowson (1990).

2 See Widdowson and Candlin (eds.) (1987–94) *Language Teaching: A Scheme for Teacher Education* where they state: 'The purpose of this scheme of books is to engage language teachers in a process of continual professional development ... We believe that advances in language teaching stem from the independent efforts of teachers in their own classrooms. This independence is not brought about by imposing fixed ideas and providing fashionable formulas. It can only occur where teachers, individually and collectively, explore principles and experiment with techniques.'

8.2   Four significant areas of teacher training

The pedagogical changes proposed in this book require a widening of
the teacher's area of responsibility. The four areas covered by teacher
training are:

- knowledge of the foreign language
- methodology
- techniques for language acquisition
- personal and interpersonal dimensions

These four areas are now examined, but the fourth is explored in
more detail.

8.2.1   Knowledge of the foreign language

Secondary and tertiary education provide teachers with an intellectual grasp of the language, its syntax and morphology, as well as
some understanding of the culture of the countries in which it is
spoken. Learners, both as teachers or students, can then acquire
practical information related to the language and culture through
visits to the country where it is spoken, and through direct contact
with the people who speak it.

In traditional teaching at secondary level, the linguistic content
required in order to complete the course is largely set out in advance
in the course book, and can be revised by the teacher before each lesson begins. In LPD, by contrast, the animator must respond spontaneously to the participants' needs for expression. This requires a
highly developed command of the language, with fluency, flexibility,
and an ability to be creative in the foreign language. Training animators in LPD techniques enables some of them to acquire a much
greater facility in the foreign language as well as flexibility in their
approach to teaching.

8.2.2   Methodology

This area is surveyed in Chapters 1 and 2. It touches upon the very
foundations of our concept of teaching and learning a language. It
also involves the 'how' of our objectives: how we teach, how we
approach the language, how the learner acquires it. It leads to
building strategies which underpin the task of teaching.

The LPD approach implies a change of attitude on the part of
teachers. We can no longer take refuge in the textbook; we have

instead to distance ourselves from the solid ground of the familiar and predictable where everything has been planned in advance. We leave the domain of what can be measured scientifically. We can no longer delude ourselves with the belief that learners only learn what we teach them. We relinquish the illusion that we are all-powerful. In LPD, teachers can use methods based on creative and stimulating doubt, in which only the frame is pre-planned but in which the language is live and expressed by living people.

Being in the teacher's position of intellectual prestige may give rise to feelings of superiority. We need to avoid that danger and dedicate our knowledge to the service of learners, entering into a partnership where our students' personalities are involved as much as our own.

Obviously, our position as teachers enables us to exercise a certain pressure on students, especially in schools where we can oblige them to learn. But such an attitude can have disastrous effects on students and on the development of intellectual curiosity. More than anything else, such an attitude reveals an inability to interest students in our material, to motivate them. We risk ruining their natural curiosity and pleasure in finding out for themselves, and in developing their own self-awareness and self-esteem through their experiences of learning.

8.2.3   Techniques for language acquisition

Teachers should have at their disposal a variety of techniques and activities suited to the interests and abilities of participants, and which will encourage them to express themselves. These should be combined to form a coherent package. For this to be possible, it is often necessary to develop the teacher's own creative skills.

Some teachers are uneasy about focusing too strongly on a creative approach because it may make them aware of their own lack of creativity. They naturally hesitate before using procedures with which they feel uncomfortable. But how can teachers help students unlock their creative potential if they are not in touch with their own? At the beginning of teacher training courses, teachers may occasionally be heard to say 'My students aren't creative!'; in some cases they are simply blaming students for their own problems.

My personal belief is that every teacher and every participant can be encouraged to be creative; the central task is to unlock that creativity. Failure may occur because of the teacher's limitations, because a technique was tried too soon, because insufficient attention was paid to the person's rhythm, or simply because the teacher was not able to get through to the learners on that occasion.

Those 'teaching' creativity have to be creative too and have continually to adjust procedures to suit the participants. This necessitates sensitivity and flexibility in introducing exercises at the right time and in the right way. It is also necessary to achieve a satisfactory balance between the teacher and the procedures used, between who he or she is and how he or she works.

Belief in the people one works with and in what one is doing is an indispensable component of creativity. If a teacher does not believe in the approach, his or her commitment and expectations will be out of step with what is achieved; if little creativity is expected from learners and modest results are expected from one's own work, an inner conflict is likely. This may lead to resistance on the part of the teacher which unconsciously reduces, and can even stifle, the creativity and spontaneity of the class. Some teachers need to see positive signs of creativity in participants in order to develop a different attitude towards its energizing effects. Only then do they have a different relationship with participants, no longer seeing them in terms of their limitations but acknowledging their potential and their inner richness. Training in the use of creativity and imagination for teaching therefore requires that teachers be brought into contact with their own strengths.

8.2.4 Personal and interpersonal dimensions

When teaching focuses directly on the learner, the teacher has increasingly to develop self-examination, and to improve his or her knowledge of communication structures and types of relationship. There must be an awareness of transfers and counter-transfers, projections, worries, fears, and personal vulnerabilities in teaching situations. There must be strong and purposeful contact with their pedagogical intentions, hopes, and dreams; that is, with the deep conscious and unconscious aims underlying the task of teaching.

The communicative aspect of LPD makes it particularly important that the teacher's relational stereotypes be decoded because as animator he or she is directly and personally involved. Both the imaginary and the real are the subjects of the group's expression, and teachers and learners are both directly and symbolically involved in the process of learning. The LPD approach to a foreign language and how it is communicated to participants presupposes a developing relationship between all the individuals concerned.

Interpersonal relationships are at the heart of the teaching profession and teachers must be brought to an understanding of the possibility of a major transformation in attitudes and behaviour, the knowledge of what it means to be a teacher and what teaching methods imply. We cannot behave as if our actions were free of personal consequences just because they are not always seen in a direct causal relationship. It is dangerous to play down the harm caused by inappropriate attitudes or behaviour in teaching, on the grounds that such problems are so complex that there is no point in trying to deal with them.

Once again, the illusion of an impersonal attitude sometimes favoured by those in classical teaching circles is called into question. We cannot simply confine our roles to choosing the subject-matter or the best way of transmitting it, because teaching, even traditional teaching, implies a relationship with the learners; it is the nature of this relationship that has a determining influence, not only on learners' acquisition of the language, but also on their personal development. Let us consider both briefly.

Influence on learning a language

How much interest students have in a subject will often depend on their relationship with the teacher. This is especially true in language teaching, where emotions and relationships are so important. We can sharpen or blunt their curiosity in the foreign language, and indeed their intellectual curiosity as a whole. Our impact can be decisive. In the examples of LPD in practice (Chapters 5 and 6) there are numerous instances which illustrate the positive influence of empathetic teaching.

Influence on personal development

How we teach can either encourage or stifle particular patterns of communication and relationship. We can reinforce or help to resolve certain types of pathological relationship. The analytical and Gestalt terms for those most commonly encountered in our profession are:

- *introjection*: adopting the feelings, values, or ideas of other people;
- *projection*: refusing to recognize our own feelings and preferring to attribute them to others, e.g. accusing someone else of being aggressive when the aggression is actually coming from us;
- *retroflection*: taking on the effects of an emotion which is related to another person, e.g. channelling feelings of aggression against oneself by means of self-punishment or self-denial;

– *confluence*: lack of awareness of differences and barriers between one-self and others, e.g. assuming that other people want what we want.

The way we teach can give students more confidence in themselves and in their capacity for expression. Or it can disturb them profoundly.

The narrow functional and hierarchical relationship which forms the model in much teacher training is replaced in LPD by an open and empathetic relationship. Empathy is defined as 'The capacity for putting oneself in the other person's place, for feeling what he feels' (Richaudeau 1975: 28). It entails a movement towards the other person and is based on a welcoming attitude and an acceptance of the other personality, whatever the differences. The double technique, which plays a key role in LPD, together with various exercises in vocal and verbal listening, makes an important contribution to the development of this attitude.

A balance between our way of being and of doing is necessary in language teaching, which is, after all, an essentially communicative subject. As teachers, we often experience an echo which dates back to our acquisition of our own first language.

We are no longer the sole directors of the pedagogic process; we teach along with our learners and continue our own personal development as individuals among them; the attitudes and aptitudes we ask the participants to develop are also part of our own evolutionary progress. So the class contributes to our own evolution. Animators and participants learn to know each other using the reciprocal and reflexive sense of 'know'.

8.2.5   Influence of these areas on each other

The four areas of teacher training (8.2) influence each other:

a. Someone who only has a sound knowledge of the language (8.2.1) can be trapped or isolated in intellectual understanding which is inflexible and which cannot be transmitted to others.

b. A teacher who gives priority to developing methodological knowledge (8.2.2) can be a good theoretician but may be a mediocre practitioner.

c. A good technician (8.2.3) with no overall understanding of aims, suitable methodology, or evaluation can disrupt the acquisition process through a lack of coherence in what he or she does. The communicative approach has suffered a great deal from this lack of coherence.

d. If the teacher gives too much emphasis to the relational side of teaching, he or she may be accepted as understanding and pleasant yet fail to achieve his or her pedagogical aims (8.2.4). I would not ask an architect to build my house just because I like him or because he takes the time to listen to me.

If the teacher finds it difficult to relate to learners, however good the pedagogical aims may be, they will not succeed and will not have the desired resonance. Sound methodology even when accompanied by good techniques will not have the right impact if the teacher does not perceive and tune into what is happening in the group and fails to take a lead from the participants.

An imbalance between the four areas can also lead to serious disturbances: lack of quality in method or practice can be a source of misunderstanding and dissatisfaction. The same can happen with a style which calls for a large measure of initiative from the participants but is led by someone who lacks flexibility and fails to acquire a good understanding of the group.

Each area can also have a positive influence on another. Giving teachers techniques to stimulate communication in the class can have an impact on teachers themselves, and they may reconsider methodological concepts as a result.

The perception of the need to develop all four areas depends on the teaching approach and objectives. A pedagogy based exclusively on teaching and transmitting intellectual understanding does not reveal the need for developing the relational aspect to the same extent as a pedagogy directed towards the development of behaviours, attitudes, and aptitudes necessary for communication in the foreign language. LPD, then, because of its particular concept of language acquisition and working procedures, requires that its animators be trained more thoroughly than is customary on more traditional teacher training courses. Because of the deliberate focus on the animator's influence on the personal development of learners, LPD aims towards higher professional standards for language teachers.

For adults in particular, a decision to return to study a language in class may include a wish to overcome frustrations felt at school, or to resume some form of intellectual development. More may be at stake than simply learning the language. It is frightening to experience people dropping out after a few lessons and to reflect on how many opportunities are therefore wasted.

I am sceptical about institutions which purport to train teachers in a limited number of hours, on the grounds that they are native speakers or have a certain mastery of the language. Whatever type of teaching we practice, we have a great responsibility and our training must reflect the weight of that responsibility.

8.3 Objectives of relational training

LPD distinguishes three main objectives in relational training: listening, expression, and acceptance of oneself and others.

8.3.1 Listening

Listening to oneself

Some teachers listen too much to themselves rather than to their students. 'You aren't listening to me!' is a typical lament of this kind of teacher. Other teachers talk all the time! They use their speech to implore 'Recognize me!'. Others demand 'Understand me!' possibly a sign of lack of recognition and importance in their lives outside the classroom. Others are deeply frightened by silence, experiencing it as a threat or a vacuum they have to fill with as many words as possible.

Speech which conceals something often suggests an underlying need to rediscover how to listen to oneself as a prior step to being understood by, and understanding, other people.

We cannot work with others without learning to be in tune with ourselves; we do not leave our personal attitudes and preoccupations behind when we enter our professional world. Our teaching reflects who we are. However, our work can have a compensatory function, and we can develop new attitudes in the light of our experiences in the classroom or staffroom.

It is a matter of how we see ourselves, of becoming aware of what is happening inside us when we do something, of understanding better our behaviour and types of relationship, of grasping what motivates us, our hopes and sometimes the illusions which come with them. It is also a matter of being aware of the various defence mechanisms we use, the images which surround us, the reactions which hold us back or paralyse us. It is a matter of experiencing our teaching by listening to ourselves. Listening to ourselves is not only the basis for better self-perception and self-knowledge, but also for listening to other people; we become more sensitive to other people's needs and desires, empathize with them, begin a dialogue between inner worlds.

Listening to others

Each student wants to be listened to, understood, accepted, and recognized. But some of us have selective hearing, in the sense that we listen only to the content of what we teach; anything to do with relationships is ignored, or reaches us in a very diluted form.

There is something paradoxical about teaching a language, which is after all teaching communication, if we do not know how to listen and find understanding difficult. Understanding what a person is saying includes understanding that person, respecting him or her and encouraging self-expression. Perceiving and accepting differences opens the way to genuine dialogue.

In LPD, we use communication exercises which give participants skills to listen to the other person sensitively. These lead to a perception of both what is said and what is really meant. It makes it possible to listen to the other person at a deeper level of listening, which in turn opens the way to another level of communication.

8.3.2   The expression of self

LPD teacher training sessions deliberately focus on personal development; some animators begin by referring to themselves in a way which is carefully thought out and controlled. Later, they can express themselves in a much more spontaneous manner. They have rediscovered the use of a language which expresses themselves naturally.

As a means of encouraging rapport between hearing and expression, LPD often uses exercises in which trainee teachers begin by listening to how their bodies feel. For some of them, expressing these feelings can be a first step towards complete, confident expression. Later, we may ask them to begin in the same way, concentrating on their body's sensitivities but now making contact with emotions they associate with these feelings; this seems to help them learn to become aware of meaning in their expression.

Another possibility is to use the world of our imagination, through which we can express ourselves symbolically, protected by the fact that, although our speech may not reveal completely and directly what is really happening within, we can become aware of the significance for us of what is being symbolically expressed. Little by little we recover our capacity for expression and begin to risk talking about ourselves without feeling exposed or insecure. We can give an identity to what we feel, and experience what helps us to find our position in relation to others. This opens the way to personal restructuring through self-expression.

Developing the capacity to express oneself is essential for our psychological well-being. A large part of the problems found in therapy stem from the fact that clients cannot put their feelings into words. Re-discovering a capacity for expression means we can begin to master our problems. The pedagogy of languages has an important contribution to make in this area.

8.3.3 Accepting oneself and others

Acceptance of individuality in others leads to a self-definition of oneself as an individual in relation to other people; it can lead us sometimes to say 'no' to others, which may be a way of saying 'yes' to ourselves. It means accepting ourselves with all our defects and limitations. It means accepting the paradoxes, contradictions, and antagonisms within us, and being open to criticism in a profession where we are inevitably vulnerable and exposed to value-laden criticism and to fantasies.

So, we are forced to distance ourselves from the traditional model of the teacher, which is inherent, sometimes unconsciously, in our minds. We can now make a healthy distinction between what we do and what we are, in a profession where the two are sometimes confused, in the same way that the student who works well is described as being 'good'. A meaningful acceptance of individuality offers the chance to develop a different type of contact with oneself, another chance to be oneself. Self-acceptance is a necessary condition for being receptive to others and for accepting others as they are.

Being as ready to accept ourselves as we are ready to accept others helps us to find a style of teaching which goes with our personality and constitutes the basis of our autonomy. Why encourage learners to become autonomous in the foreign language if we ourselves have not reached autonomy in our own ability to express ourselves?

8.3.4 How we relate to wishes

In relational work, I distinguish three often confused areas of wishing: perception, expression, and realization. Each corresponds to the three training objectives described above.

Perception of wishes

Listening to ourselves means, among other things, listening to what we want. As teachers we are so used to listening outwards, towards other people, that we sometimes find it difficult to turn inwards, to listen and understand ourselves. Our profession is full of 'giving children' (Miller 1983), in this case, referring to those of us who are so used to listening to and going along with what others want that we lose sight of our own needs and wishes.

Some teachers think they should aspire only to what is attainable. They are no longer in touch with their wishes and restrict themselves to those material satisfactions they know they can realize—a casual fatalism characterized by remarks such as 'Anyway, it's not possible, so there's no point even thinking about it'. As intellectuals, we can always find good reasons for not listening to ourselves—'It's not important, it was just a childish whim ...'. This can develop into a chronic affective deafness in our personal and professional lives. To be in touch with our wishes is to be in touch with an essential part of ourselves. It can allow us to have a better understanding of where we stand in our affective existence. Listening to our own wishes is an indispensable measure of our psychological health.

Expression of wishes

Here is a short story:

> They had been living together for fifty years. For fifty years she had made him breakfast every morning, cutting the bread rolls in half and giving him the top, crusty half to eat; she thought he liked it best. On the morning of their fiftieth anniversary she timidly asked 'Would you mind if I had the top half this morning?' Quite astonished, he looked at her and said, 'Of course not, I prefer the bottom half!'.

When some of us become aware of our wishes we are too frightened to give them expression because we think they are impossible. This problem arises from a common confusion between the expression of a wish and the expectation of its fulfilment. It has its origins in childhood; children find it difficult to see that their wishes may not be fulfilled and are consequently hurt when they are not. Expressing our wishes, even if they cannot be realized, often helps us to come to terms with them: instead of denying or suppressing them we can understand how they are made up and confront them in an adult way. When a wish relates to another person, expressing it often changes something in the relationship with that person and helps him or her to understand. Expressing a wish allows us to effect the first step in achieving it; hiding it is not just foregoing the right to dream, but to an important part of reality.

Realization of wishes

Some wishes cannot be realized because of objective circumstances and conditions, but we may be able to attain them symbolically by bridging the gap between our inner and external worlds. It is also part of our condition as adults that we come to terms with unrealistic wishes but without denying their existence, recognizing that we do not inhabit a magic world where everything is possible, and that we may have to abandon the hope of realizing, or we may have to modify them.

Professional wishes

Knowing what we are aiming for and what motivates us as teachers makes it possible to create a link between our inner and our professional lives. The main part of our professional training will not have taken place when we were studying to become teachers, but it will also have developed imperceptibly through our childhood and school years. The teaching of our family life, the lessons taught at home and school are the deep roots of our pedagogy.

Our professional wishes and ambitions have developed in relation to that early education, including the wish to do as well as or better than those who trained us, who served as our pedagogical reference points.

What wishes have we failed to respond to? What unrealized dreams slumber on, lost within the workings of the school system or buried in chalk dust? What ideas have been stifled by the daily grind? We may need to readjust the image we have been given of our profession. Sometimes our illusions need updating, like those in relationships who refuse to see that their partner no longer fits the image they had of them at the beginning: they continue to harbour the same hopes and therefore the same disappointments. We must learn to adjust to current situations and alter aims accordingly.

Renewing aims and becoming increasingly self-aware does not mean a new behaviour pattern for each new learning project. This would only lead to a manipulation of our students. It is, rather, a matter of listening to oneself more attentively and defining our wishes in a context which is sympathetic to others while at the same time reflecting a deep acceptance of ourselves and others.

8.4　Self-image as teachers

In coming into contact with ourselves we also come into contact with the images, myths, and fantasies which inhabit our inner universe.

We can prise open the door to that universe.

In our profession, we are inevitably exposed to the watchful eyes of classes, individual learners, colleagues, senior managers and, in schools, parents. We may find ourselves torn between:

- our image of ourselves;
- what we want to be (our wished-for image) or do not want to be;
- the image of ourselves we receive back, directly or unconsciously, from classes and individual learners;
- who we really are.

We may be prepared to accept remarks which relate to how we would like to see ourselves (our wished-for image). However, even if we are aware of our shortcomings, we do not always appreciate having them pointed out to us.

Remarks which reveal a gap between our self-image and how others see us can be harder to accept. This sort of confrontation can lead to an immediate chill in classroom relationship because our self-image goes very deep and criticisms can be gravely damaging. It is our perception of ourselves that is on trial, and this can give rise to agonizing doubts about our identities. 'Who am I if I am not who I think I am?' In other words, professional criticism can have an impact that goes far beyond the question of our professional identity.

Work on personal development can bring about changes in our perception of ourselves. It can help us to see other people's reactions as opportunities to correct our self-image and see ourselves from a fresh perspective, while not undermining our overall view of who we are. We also become used to distinguishing between those messages which are directed specifically at us and those which are projections or transfers, realizing that it is sometimes possible to reflect part of the criticism back to the person who is making it in a movement of self-protection. Enlarging self-perception through the image reflected by others can help our own acceptance of differences as teachers.

Sometimes teachers are locked into an image imposed on them from outside. One participant in a teacher training group became aware of other people's narrow and confining image of her. Gradually, she made efforts to distance herself from their image of her in order to decide how much she would or would not accept, and so was able to find more of her true self.

In some teacher training courses we use a technique in which the participants become statues in an organized tableau; one participant arranges the others in particular attitudes or poses to create what is, to begin with, a static image of themselves teaching. The participant then creates an ideal self-image. The transition from one scene to the other enables the participants to identify what separates them from their objectives, what direction they are going in, and what criteria they might use to measure their performance. Feedback from fellow participants to these 'tableaux' can help them begin to modify and enlarge their perception of themselves—within a reassuring environment.

8.5 Myths teachers have about teachers

We do not enter the classroom as innocents; we are carriers of myths conferred by our educational history or which we have nurtured inside us; these myths foster what we try to do in our personal and professional lives, as well as our illusions and disappointments. We will briefly examine some myths.

Pygmalion

Pygmalion is the first myth that comes to mind (Kaes *et al.* 1979: 42–43, 66). It is a story-line which provides a model for 'fashioning' another person to become the object of our desires and plans. The learner is considered to be like clay in our hands. We have the fantasy not just of being able to change a person but of creating a complementary, or even idealized, image of ourselves. This makes the exercise of teaching all the more demanding, and correspondingly disappointing if we fail. The learner has to become an extension of ourselves, of our hopes, and of those things we could not do ourselves. We thus live out our wishes by proxy. The Pygmalion myth can be extended into another myth of Frankenstein proportions, a desire to create an intellectual monster whose only criteria for private fulfilment are intellectual achievements.

Parenting

It is a familiar phenomenon in family life for parents to want their children to take over from them. They invest in their children the hopes they were unable to realize. Disappointment is all the stronger when the children do not share these wishes and ambitions, and do not come up to their expectations. Many teachers see themselves as parents to their students.

There is something narcissistic about wanting to see oneself in someone else, or wanting to create an idealized self-image in another person. In such a situation, teachers feel learners' mistakes more directly because they not only reflect our professional competence, but perhaps more importantly because we want them to fulfil our personal desires, because of the creation of the image of ourselves which we transpose on to them.

As teachers of younger children, we partly take the place of the family; going to school is often the first important separation from the family. Two functions symbolize our role as stand-in parents, the foster parent, and the representative of authority.

As teachers, we try to provide intellectual and social nourishment. In doing so, we respond to the wish to transmit what we know. But there may be another strong underlying motivation; we take on the role of foster parent.

Our desire to be helpful can go too far: it can lead us to force-feed learners with intellectual facts, and kill off enthusiasm for the diet we are recommending. This is why we often meet adults who have no wish to read the books they were taught at school. By forcing learners to study these works instead of developing an appetite for literature, we often achieve precisely the opposite effect. This wish to 'feed minds' can be so strong that some teachers say 'My students are tearing me apart', 'The work's killing me', 'They're bleeding me to death'. Teaching then becomes an act of sacrifice.

What drives us to give so much, especially when those on the receiving end would prefer us not to? What needs are we responding to, or attempting to respond to, when we teach?

Sometimes we are trying to give something we would like to have had during our own schooldays. We often come into the profession wanting to do better than the teachers we had at school. We may want to fill something inside us for which we still feel the need. We expect learners to recognize and be grateful for the effort and self-denial we impose on ourselves. We are sometimes too affected by learners' criticisms; like a disappointed parent we may say 'After all I've done for them!'

It is hardly surprising that learners are not always aware of what we think they need, and feel the gift we want to give them as an unwelcome imposition. We are deciding what they want, not listening and responding to their needs. Failing to identify the learner's own needs gives rise to misunderstandings and disappointments. Becoming aware of *whose* need is being satisfied also helps us to recognize our personal need for gratitude, and to understand that we should not expect learners to gratify needs which should find their satisfaction elsewhere.

In LPD, we find this carry-over of need translated into some aspects of sessions related to self-development. Here is an example: Lucia strokes another participant's hair in a 'tableau' which represents a family; it gradually becomes clear to the participants that she wants the other woman to stroke her hair, i.e. she is projecting on to someone else her own wishes.

It is important in training to help those teachers who have a tendency to give what they themselves want to receive, to focus on their own needs and wishes. Many of us lose the habit of expressing what we want, and live in a world of 'magic requests'. Like the child who expects a parent to know what he or she needs without asking for it; some of us imagine that a wish will be as obvious to others as it is to ourselves. What is more, because we strive to guess at other people's unspoken needs, we expect the same attitude from others. We may have the impression that people do not identify our own needs and wishes because they do not want to. In such situations failure becomes a source of great tension.

Some teachers make few demands for fear of being refused. Personal development groups help them to make demands and accept that risk of refusal. Fantasies of rejection can be clarified if, after they have expressed the reasons they believe lie behind that 'no', the person concerned clarifies them.

When a person takes on the function of teacher, he or she becomes the representative of law and order, creating a framework which gives reassurance to learners by providing protection from any potential excesses of the class and from fears of chaos. In this way, the teacher contributes to both the structuring and working of the group. The teacher takes on the role of a protective parent which can easily lead to a 'pedagogic paternalism'. The teacher is the representative of power, controlling learners as well as the standards and routines of the system that employs him or her. Most teachers find strength in both this hierarchical position and the prestige of having superior knowledge.

Locked into this function of the all-powerful parent, a teacher sometimes shows tendencies towards absolutism, reflected, for example, in assumptions of infallibility and in being impervious to all criticism from students; permanently on guard against anything that might reveal his or her limitations, inadequacies, weaknesses, or mistakes. This illusion of power is also seen in the hope that students will learn all that is taught. Once disappointed in this expectation, a teacher may become isolated with his or her teaching objectives and extreme frustration can set in, especially if a lot of time and effort has been invested. This expectation is a guarantee of eventual disappointment. Such teachers imagine themselves in a world where no weakness is allowed; they come to teacher training courses with a very strong need to develop their knowledge and power but with little patience for weaknesses or shortcomings.

Where aspects of a teacher's parental role as helper and nourisher may cause unhappiness for the teacher, the role of the all-powerful parent can represent a real danger for students. A teacher in this role might want to realize a range of objectives at whatever cost to students. It is very important that a teacher understands what the profession means for him or her, and where his or her compulsion to teach could lead. In Teacher Development courses, by asking trainee teachers to present an ideal participant or class, we may make them partly aware of their motives where other people are concerned.

The myth of the surrogate parents is one way of making contact with those who fashioned us—our first teachers, near and distant members of the family, grandparents lost in family history, rejected family members who became our unconscious models (I owe this observation to a work of systemic analysis by Bert Hellinger, RFA). These are real or mythical heroes of our childhood, models who have given some shape to our own world of learning. Encountering these models and their messages helps us to understand what lies behind our own behaviour as teachers.

The Don Juan

We examine the teacher's wish to seduce, in other words, to please and be loved but also to be recognized and appreciated. This shows itself in different ways. In one way, the teacher tries to pull the class along in his or her wake, like the Pied Piper of Hamelin, behaving as the leader who risks leaving the class exhausted behind him. In another way, as the conqueror, the class is the battleground and the teacher sets out to assault and possess it, talking grandly of 'my' group, and 'my' students.

We see the pedagogic Eros in its charming form: the seduction may be intellectual—after all, the teacher has a brilliant mind—or focus on the emotions, when the teacher becomes attractive, even spell-binding. When such a teacher asks classes for feedback, he or she wants to hear approval of the methods and strategies used. The teacher is seeking, in a roundabout way, personal confirmation and praise and will react very badly to any responses which express doubt.

Many other mythical figures inhabit teachers' inner worlds, including Prometheus, Don Quixote, Dr Jeckyll and Mr Hyde, the

Twins (symbols of the wish for completeness), Zorro the Avenger, the Missionary, real-life heroes, and others taken from fairy-tales and books we remember from our childhood. I have chosen those that seem more common and more relevant. As teachers we have found many other examples not described above.

8.6 Training LPD animators

In order to give a clearer idea of the LPD approach to training, a description of the training of animators in the Mainz LPD Centre is given below. We suppose that teachers have a good enough knowledge of the target language to be able to teach it, so our training concentrates on methodological, technical, and relational aspects.

Sensitization

We recommend that anyone unfamiliar with LPD techniques should attend at least one intensive one-week course, or two weekend courses, as a participant, working in a language of which they have little or no prior knowledge. This brings them into direct contact with our approach and they can experience the effects of LPD procedures themselves and observe the effects on other participants. They can thus begin to understand the techniques and to identify what attitudes might be required of the animators.

Basic training

The main objective of a training course is to transmit the basic techniques of linguistic psychodramaturgy in a course lasting six weekends of three days each, spread over six months. Between each weekend the animators train in smaller groups with students or friends willing to act as participants. Learning LPD takes place on three levels:

The physical dimension

Since the body is our receiving antenna, exercises in body sensitivity are proposed to participants. Participants learn to get themselves more in tune with their bodies and the reactions and messages that come from them. This is done by a combination of exercises in relaxation, breathing, and sensory perception. They are also sensitized to the psychological influences of nearness and distance: this is particularly important in LPD, since we work without any furniture and the area of space a person occupies or distances between people can be important.

The affective dimension
The affective objectives have already been described elsewhere in this book: listening to the self, to one's own needs and fears and expectations; listening to others, and awareness of other people's ways of relating and communicating, their attitudes and behaviour patterns; expression of the self. Personal development takes place, focusing on what happens in groups when these future animators have been trained in LPD techniques.

The intellect
Training involves the theory of LPD methodology (Chapters 1 and 2) and how it differs from traditional teaching (B. Dufeu 1985) or other types of teaching (Dufeu 1987, 1992).

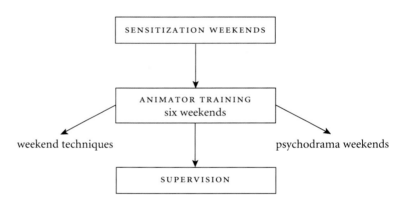

FIGURE 9 *The LPD training programme*

Follow-up training

Teachers can follow up this basic training with technical and personal development. After the initial weekends, teachers work on any LPD techniques they found difficult to use. They are also brought up-to-date with any new developments, such as new warm-ups and new exercises. We also try each time to go a little deeper into a discussion of theoretical points.

The personal development sessions deal with any relational problems encountered during the course, as well as any problems trainees bring to the class or which emerge during sessions. Since personal development has an effect on how we work, especially on sensitization of oneself and others, we do not try to make an artificial division between the personal and the professional. It is in some senses a matter of a relational supervision. Some individuals take part in LPD basic training courses and personal development, at the same time. These courses are also open to teachers who follow other teaching approaches. We also arrange supervisions, during which an animator from the LPD Centre monitors the work of one team over one or two weekends or a week, takes part in preparing the course, and observes the relationship of teachers with participants, how they present and lead the exercises, and how well the correlation between warm-ups and exercises actually works.

Diplomas are not given to animators until this supervised stage has been successfully completed and they satisfy the criteria set down by experienced LPD trainers.

8.7 Conclusion

A number of other topics in relational training are also covered in these programmes. These include the relation of the teacher to the language taught and those who speak it. We also deal with the hopes and fears of the teacher, for example, when criticism offers a threat to self-image. The potential for conflict in a profession noted for the pursuit of harmony is likewise covered. Some teachers over-value intellectual activity, or are disappointed by the decline in social status and what is seen as de-professionalization of teachers. Others consider teaching to be the fulfilment of a social mission; this can lead to a sense of sacrifice, emphasized by frustration when learners do not respond. The teaching profession sometimes has to satisfy a need for personal security but, partly because of feelings of vulnerability due to being continually 'in the spotlight', this often leads to the use of self-defence strategies. Finally, the desire for more knowledge has to respond to the wish to complete the task which is felt. But, since this is impossible, there is inner unhappiness and a permanent quest for perfection.

The task of teaching is never-ending; we are engaged in a continual process of evolution. LPD training deliberately reflects this. The importance of this work lies not just in the positive pedagogic results obtained, but in the changes of attitude and behaviour of teachers. We can develop our capacity to be more open and spontaneous, and so to be more ourselves.

9 Personal relations in teacher training

In order to illustrate some aspects of relational teacher training, this chapter deals with exercises which allow teachers to become sensitized to the emotional dimensions of the pedagogical relationship.

Afterwards, some of the problems encountered by LPD animators in the course of their work, are described in order to explain more precisely how the experience expresses itself in the world of teaching.

9.1 Exercises in sensitizing to emotional aspects of teaching

There is a danger for teachers of taking on a psychotherapeutic role because they belong to the 'helping' professions such as doctors, psychologists, and nurses, and they have a great tendency to want to help or to avoid their own problems by helping others. Teachers are often 'helpless helpers' (Schmidbauer 1977).

Having trained doctors, psychologists, and teachers in psychodrama, we feel that trainees are the most dangerous at the beginning of their training, when they think they have enough experience to work with this method. Even when you have the competence to work with a psychological approach, it is important to make clear what you are doing, and to be supervised. Undertaking psychological work involves a long period of self-development, during which participants have to confront their own problems, attitudes, and strategies, with training over several years, and supervision of their work in an environment free from distractions.

In this chapter, we will give some examples of psychodrama involving teachers. The courses were advertised as self-development courses during which psychodrama would be used as a way of developing self-awareness.

Development of inner hearing: in double

Participants form pairs and talk together for a few minutes on topics such as what they hope for and expect from the course, any worries they may have about it or their first impressions. It is important to distinguish between hopes and expectations: I may have hopes for a course of study but may not expect them to be fulfilled, but expectations are possible. Explain to participants that they must be good listeners and remember what is said to them. They should also be able to identify what their partner is expressing while they are giving information. They are warned that they will be asked to tell others what was discussed.

The group comes together again. The animator asks for a pair to volunteer to share their discussions with the class. One of the pair stands behind his or her partner (the protagonist) and tries to share with the class not only what was said during their conversation but also what they felt their partner expressed. The 'double' talks in the first person, as if in the partner's place. Other members of the class then come, in turn, to stand behind the protagonist, saying whatever they think he or she could have expressed. Afterwards, the protagonist provides whatever corrections or explanations he or she feels may be necessary.

Such exercises encourage an 'inner hearing' of other people, an awareness of the difference between what is said and what is expressed—an important distinction in communication. They can make us aware that when we start out on a new adventure, such as a new course of study, we have not only hopes and expectations, but also doubts and fears about the course and ourselves.[1]

Sensitization to imaginary projections: the crystal ball

We use this particular exercise at the start of a teacher training course before participants have got to know each other. An animator explains that one participant (the protagonist) is to be the centre of attention for a few minutes. Everyone else can give free rein to their imagination and say whatever they imagine, but do not know, about that person, for example, what they like to do in their spare time, their family background, past life, hopes, etc. The animator explains that whatever other participants say during this exercise may be important to the protagonist, because he or she will realize the images and impressions others may have. In a teacher training session impressions can be stated explicitly. We now ask for a participant to volunteer to be the protagonist.

The protagonist must try to keep a poker face while the others are talking so as not to give any clues about the accuracy or value of what is being said. It seems to us important to stress that an exercise like this may appear to focus on the protagonist, but often reveals a great

[1] This doubling exercise is taken from the psychodrama tradition.

deal about the other participants who are busily expressing feelings and attitudes while they are giving information and ideas. When the class has finished talking, the protagonist can describe his or her feelings and impressions if they want to, and correct or add to what has been said.

This exercise tends to have quite an impact on participants; they are amazed to see how much they communicate about themselves without explicitly saying anything. This helps to sensitize the group to unconscious messages we send and to projections or transfers about ourselves in our personal or professional lives.[2]

Sensitizing to the individual's behaviour: the car

Participants form pairs, A and B. A closes his or her eyes and B stands behind putting both hands on A's shoulders or shoulder blades. B then 'drives' A around the room, taking care that A does not bump into anything or anyone. The exercise is carried out in complete silence so that any messages are conveyed entirely by body language. After a few minutes, the partners reverse roles. They then choose other partners from the class.

As the exercise develops, we ask participants to give increasingly subtle signals to the person they are 'driving', for example, steering with a single finger instead of both hands. In a particularly responsive group, it may be possible to ask participants, towards the end of the exercise, to try to steer each other without touch, simply by walking behind their partner and thinking about the direction to take.

Variation: the imaginary journey
This exercise follows the same approach but, instead of steering a partner from behind, the 'driver' walks alongside and takes the other person on an imaginary journey up stairs, through a low tunnel, into a wood, and so on, in complete silence.[3]

These two exercises can also help participants to become aware of how they lead a group, how they respond to being 'driven' by someone else. Needless to say, it is a most effective exercise for building group trust.

Exercises in Chapter 5 such as *Hand mirror* (5.2.2) or *A forest of sounds* (5.2.2), can be used to the same effect.

Empathy training: posing

A participant volunteers and comes to the centre of the room, concentrates on himself or herself, and then adopts a given pose. Two or three others take up the same position behind the first participant

2 We owe this exercise to Serge Ginger, co-founder of, and trainer in, the École Parisienne de Gestalt.

3 We owe this exercise and its variant to Augusto Boal.

but at the same time expressing what they feel when they adopt that pose. This exercise helps develop empathetic perception. The double exercise described in Chapter 5 (5.2.1) is also very effective in enhancing empathy.

Self-image, other-image: the sculptor

The principle of this exercise is taken from traditions of training for actors in the theatre.

My image of the other person

Participants form pairs, A and B. A acts as sculptor and treats B as if he or she is a block of marble. A 'sculpts' B, making B adopt a position which, in A's opinion, represents an image formed of this person as a fellow participant, or even as the animator. The roles are then reversed and B 'sculpts' A. Afterwards, partners can discuss their feelings. There may be time to form new pairs and repeat the exercise.

The counter-image

We sometimes ask the sculptors to make two sculptures of the same person. The first is the way in which he or she perceives the other; the second is the opposite of that perception. Often, the second sculpture is the more revealing of the two.[4]

4 We owe this technique to Connie Kleijn, a Dutch psychodramatist.

The ideal participant

We sometimes ask the teachers to sculpt their image of an ideal participant, or even of the most annoying participant they can think of. Afterwards, they give a fictitious name to the finished sculpture, and ask the 'model' to say what feelings they had during the sculpturing and what they feel now. This exercise can be very revealing and can sensitize teachers to how they relate to participants and what to expect from them.

Image of a professional situation: the tableau vivant

Sometimes we ask a participant to volunteer to be the protagonist and to represent his or her professional life by using other participants who they arrange in 'poses' as a 'tableau vivant'. They can state an important change they would like to make and then try to represent the change in a revised 'tableau'. The final step is to move from the 'tableau' representing the actual situation to the 'tableau' which represents an idealized image of his or her occupation and to work on the changes needed to come closer to the ideal situation.

Tensions sometimes arise between the protagonist and the characters in the 'tableau'. If they agree to it, we work together to clarify why these tensions occur.

Variation: vignette

A vignette is a scene lasting two or three minutes. As a variation of the 'tableau', we ask a protagonist to represent a difficult situation they have encountered in the past or might encounter in the future. Other participants who take part in the vignette can relate their feelings, and this helps the protagonist to find solutions or to get a new awareness of what is going on inside him or her.

9.2 Case studies from teacher training courses

These are self-development courses.

9.2.1 Relationship to the subject

How well a target language is transmitted to learners depends, among other things, on the teacher's relationship with the language and those who speak it. It is, therefore, important to be aware of what type of relationship we have with the language and the images we have of those who speak it (Feldhendler 1990).

Sometimes we ask trainers to present the subject they are teaching as a 'tableau vivant'. As a topic, we sometimes suggest 'People who have influenced my attitude to the subject'. Having done so, we then ask them to take the place of various people in the 'tableau', and to themselves portray what it means for them to be directly associated with the subject: 'I am what I teach'.

In LPD teacher training courses, the relationship with the language has emerged spontaneously on some occasions, as in the following two examples. Names of participants have been changed in the examples to protect their anonymity.

Kathrin

On a weekend course for LPD trainers, the trainers were, in small groups, learning the double technique. Kathrin was doubling Reinhold in French; I noticed that her sequence was completely lifeless and gently pointed this out to her. When the scene was repeated there was no improvement; Kathrin may have been using French words but her voice had no expression. I suggested to her that she should exchange places with Reinhold, the protagonist, putting on a 'blind' half mask and expressing herself spontaneously. She repeated the beginning of the sequence several times, trying to bring life into the words she was using, and I sensed that she was struggling against an emotional barrier: suddenly she burst into tears. She explained that she felt very embarrassed when she spoke French, the language she taught, because from the time of her first stay in the country the French used to chastise her, correcting all she said and making it clear that she could not speak French well. But, in saying this, she expressed her frustration and anger *in French*, and this gave her the opportunity to rediscover her emotional expression in the language. When she returned to her role as double, I observed that the language had taken on an entirely different quality of expression. The exercise had enabled her to make contact with repressed emotions that had prevented her from giving life to the words she was speaking.

Hanne

A similar situation took place in another teacher training group: in a mirror exercise Hanne expressed herself in her native language, German, but her head seemed to get in the way of her first language so that she spoke a neutralized form. When I pointed this out to her she said, 'My mother tongue has become a foreign language to me'. The exercise slowly revealed that during the latter years of her married life she had felt silenced and hardly spoke at all. I could not make any further progress at the time because I observed that Hanne's awareness was sufficient for the time being; I felt that the origins of her silence lay deeper. Little by little, we came to see how her expression within the training group acquired new life using exercises which let her express her bodily sensations, feelings, and emotions. The relational work of LPD helped Hanne enormously, not only with her expression, but also with her emotional life in her native language.

9.2.2 Relations with others

Next, we look at another example taken from a different LPD teacher training context which illustrates how a person's life experience can transform the meaning of an exercise.

Britta and Rolf

We were on the second weekend of a training course for LPD animators. Teachers of English, French, Italian, and German had divided into language sub-groups, and were training in a mirror exercise.

In LPD, the mirror exercise symbolically marks the stage where the participants become aware of the difference within themselves between 'self' and 'the other' and of the consequence for language of the breakdown from the fused self-other to a personalized 'me', and to 'you'.

Once the preparation for this exercise was completed, participants came together and exchanged their impressions of what they had done so far. Britta had been working as an animator with Rolf as a protagonist. She was deeply upset at something which had just happened and expressed her disappointment in a depressed voice. It emerged that Rolf had not responded very well to what she had proposed (and which, to judge from her extreme disappointment, she wanted to impose on him). She added, 'I felt a long way from myself'. She was half lying on the ground suffering from severe back pains.

With her agreement, we went more deeply into what she had been saying. She remembered that when she was small she had fallen over with a pot of jam in her hands. Although she had hurt herself badly, she was proud to have been able to take the pot, unbroken, to her mother. Put another way, she had been able to fulfil what was expected of her. (Perhaps at the same time she had learnt to prefer suffering pain to failing in her duty.)

The memory of her relationship with her mother then became more specific. Given the importance of her personal responses in what she had said, and the marked degree of attention shown by the group (which suggested to me that her problem found an echo in several other participants), I asked her if she wanted to take the process a stage further, in order to understand more fully what was happening to her. She agreed.

I then asked her to look for someone in the group who might take on the role of her mother. She glanced around the group and stopped when she saw a mask painted in dark colours hanging on the wall. The mask was made by Marie, another animator in the group, and so in this instance, its symbolic mother. Britta took down the mask and hung it on the handle of a door in the room. Following a dialogue and role-reversal using the mask to represent her mother, it emerged that her mother exercised considerable emotional pressure on Britta, demanding that she should come to see her more often and listen more attentively to her on such visits, all out of recognition (in the full sense of the word) for everything that she, mother, had done for her daughter. Britta attempted, with difficulty and guilt, to distance herself from her mother during her dialogue with the mask and not to continue to be drawn into a deeper relationship. At the end of the session, Britta decided to space out her visits in spite of her mother's powerful emotional blackmail.

The correspondence between the symbolic function of the mirror exercise and Britta's use of the mask is plain enough. She had become aware that she had made the same sorts of demands as her mother and had expected Rolf to listen to her, and adopt her own speech as his own. She transposed onto Rolf, and perhaps other students in her classes, this demand for maternal fusion.

Later, she also expressed her realization of the conflict between what she would like to be, a good animator who gives without asking for anything in return, and thus the good mother, and the emotional demands of her mother which she had interiorized but refused to accept. She was confronted by Rolf's reaction to the mirroring of these attitudes, a very different image of herself from the one she would have liked to have.

Perhaps in a more traditional training course, Britta would have returned home with the impression that it had failed her, that the LPD course had not worked in the way she had expected. On the other hand, the LPD course fulfilled its function marvellously for Rolf. An exercise viewed as successful by Britta would have been a failure for Rolf because it would have meant that he had given in to Britta's demands; he would have behaved to please her which would have entailed a sequence that would not have echoed what he really wanted to express.

The dichotomy between Britta's expectations, as shown in her proposal in the training exercise, and Rolf's desire to be free to choose between expression or non-expression, as shown in his reluctance to agree, reveals the differences in personalities which prompt us to want to express our own needs and wishes freely. Out of the training exercise a meaningful dialogue between Britta and Rolf was born.

In this example of the mirror exercise between Britta and Rolf, one can see a theme that often concerns us as teachers; we find it difficult to accept that the messages we transmit may be transformed or distorted. Frequently, in a confusion between doing and being, it is not just our words but a part of ourselves that is heard, transformed, and often distorted by the listener.

Britta's disappointment also reflects the difficulty every teacher has in coming to terms with his or her limitations. Rolf's reaction made Britta realize not only that she was not the deeply sensitive and empathetic animator she considered herself to be, but also that she must work on her ability to deal with autonomy in the classroom. This example raises a number of questions relating to exercises used in language courses:

– What kind of relationship between participants is encouraged by
the exercise I am using, immediately and potentially?
– What symbolism (illustrating, for example, self-images, social
attitudes, relationships) does it contain?
– What are my explicit, but also my hidden, pedagogical objectives?
– What is my overall approach?
– Have I achieved a balance between how I perceive my role, who I
am, and how I behave?

9.2.3   Psychodrama courses for teachers

In psychodrama, instead of talking about problems they encounter,
participants represent them dramatically. Re-enacting them helps to
understand them better. Similar dramatic portrayals are part of
teacher training courses and these enactments can have similar
therapeutic effects. Here are three examples, taken from teacher
training courses, which illustrate different kinds of emotional and
attitudinal problems that surfaced in training animators.

Marion

Marion took part in a teacher training course for teachers. It was the
second day and she presented an event that took place the week
before, and that she recalled during a group warm-up. She runs an
alternative nursery school with a colleague, and a mother had told her
that she was going to withdraw her daughter, Carola. When Marion
presented the situation we saw her almost begging the mother not to
withdraw the child because she felt that this would be very upsetting
for Carola. Gradually, it emerged that Marion identified very strongly
with Carola, and in the course of the psychodrama session Marion's
own story was revealed:

When Marion was five years old her mother died suddenly; since
she was considered to be too young, she was not allowed to attend
the funeral. What is more, the day after the funeral her grandmother
had taken her to live with her in another town. She was taken out of
her nursery school without a chance to say goodbye to her playmates.
This brutal double separation affected her deeply.

An imagined dialogue was then organized between Marion and a
participant who played the part of one of her nursery school friends
so that she could say goodbye.

At a later stage, another session enabled Marion to say goodbye to
her mother. Until then she had not been able to deal with the separation from her mother or from her young playmates. Marion now

began a period of grieving which may help her to accept separations in her life and begin to identify and gradually overcome fears associated with all forms of separation. The psychodramatic approach had a reparative and structuring effect.

Julia

Julia was taking part in a week-long personal course in development. It was the third day and she presented a scene based on her experience at work; a woman colleague had begun to take over more and more of her space after taking Julia's desk, and was now putting more and more things on the second desk Julia was now using. Julia saw her own space shrinking more and more, and although she had a growing feeling of resentment, had resigned herself to accepting the situation without protest. But she was losing all pleasure in her work. This resigned attitude reminded her suddenly of an identical attitude shown by her father and paternal grandfather, who accepted whatever happened to them.

We let her repeat the scene with her colleague, this time drawing a clear boundary round her own territory. But it was not only her physical space that she was delineating. In her dialogue, she was beginning to define her needs and desires.

Georges

During a teacher training course, Georges played out a scene that had taken place a short while before, involving his manager at work. Georges had approached him, full of smiles, before making a number of complaints. His manager had reacted all the more strongly to these complaints because he felt tricked by Georges' manner when he had entered his office.

After a role-reversal, Georges re-enacted this scene, trying to be more in touch with his feelings, and expressing how he felt about his manager's reaction; this was the source of his unhappiness. This time he began with feeling 'I' ('I was annoyed by ...') instead of the accusatory 'you' ('You should ...') which he had used in the first enactment and which had prevented him from having the dialogue with his manager he had intended. This experience helped Georges to express his feelings more directly and to have better contact with his manager. Such a change in attitude would produce noticeable improvements in his teaching as well as his personal life.

9.3 Conclusion

Some teachers will no doubt ask themselves what effect these teacher training exercises will have on participants. It is difficult to be exact because the effects are symbolic as well as direct.[5] Taking the last three examples:

Marion found it difficult not to seek bonding with her students—separation for her was difficult. It is possible that after this training Marion will be able to overcome her tendency towards over-close relations with her students and let them develop their autonomy more freely.

Julia might find that she can stand up for herself more when she disagrees with participants, or feels swamped by them. She may also learn to express her needs and desires.

Georges is learning to express himself more readily, to communicate in a way participants, colleagues, and others will find easier to understand.

But what seems to me to be the most important outcome for the three individuals and for all teacher trainers who take part in a pyschodrama course, is how they are becoming sensitized to different modes of communication, and the relationships they have with themselves, participants, colleagues, and everyone else around them. It is not only their own role plays and activities as protagonists that help to provide another perception of themselves and other people, but also the work carried out by the other participants. The psychodrama approach encourages an awareness of one's own behaviour and the origins of the positive or negative resonance of other people's behaviour. A restructuring process takes place of which those directly concerned may not be immediately aware but whose effects are noticed by those around them.

The psychodrama approach, then, results in a greater sensitivity to ourselves and other people. In a subject such as language teaching this is not just useful but indispensible.

Watch not my eyes
But where I am looking. [ZEN]

Glossary

A change of perspective affords an explanation of how certain terms have been used in this book.

dramaturgy the knowledge that helps us to understand which rules are necessary for setting up a lively action or a good drama. It involves the use of principles derived from the stage, which make drama techniques work well. In linguistic psychodramaturgy it includes adapting these principles to language learning and helping us to facilitate the setting up of an interesting action and interaction between participants. See *linguistic psychodramaturgy*.

expression see *meaning*.

learner is any person who is learning something being taught. A teacher in training is a learner. See *participant*.

learning/acquisition we agree here partly with Krashen's (1982) distinction in the context of learning a foreign language: *learning* is a conscious process in which the contents are clearly defined; *acquisition* is mostly a subconscious process or the result of this process. I have not learnt my first language, I have acquired it.

linguistic psychodramaturgy (LPD) a pedagogical approach to foreign language learning using some of the principles and techniques of *psychodrama* (a therapeutical method) and *dramaturgy*.

meaning the literal meaning of 'It is six o'clock' is connected with a certain time during the day (six hours after noon). This is called denotative meaning. The meaning of 'It is six o'clock' in the context of what is being *expressed* can be: it is very soon, too late, time to go, etc. Meaning is always related to connotations of the message, i.e. which personal resonance it has for me. This is known as connotative or expressive meaning and it is expressed through intonation and forms of paralinguistic expression.

memorization/retention *memorization* is the conscious process of learning something by heart and storing it in one's memory. *Retention* is the fact that the information is in the memory. This can be achieved through an act of memorization or through other processes. Many events in one's life have been stored without learning them and many personal facts (who my neighbours are, who my best friend is ...) continue to be known without memorizing them. In traditional teaching, memorizing of content and rules plays a major role, which is not the case with LPD.

participant is a member of a group of individuals who participate in the activities of the group and relate as individuals with the other members of the group. Through this participation he or she joins in the learning activity. In practising expression during this activity, he or she will acquire the target language (which becomes a means of expression, not the aim of the course) often without being directly conscious of it. See *learner*.

psychodrama a therapeutical approach to personal development and mental illness, created by Jacob Levy Moreno (1889–1974). Instead of discussing difficulties, problems, or desires, clients enact them with the help of the other members of the group who play the roles of the persons implicated in the situations. It is a therapy which operates in and through action. See *linguistic psychodramaturgy*.

psychodramaturgy see *linguistic psychodramaturgy*.

retention see *memorization*.

sequence a set of language components which constitutes a unity of expression. It may be a sequence of two or three minutes expressing the impressions of a participant. It may be a short dialogue between two participants. The sequence in LPD is repeated in different ways, which allows for a development of expression by participants and a better mastery and retention of the new elements of the language.

symbolic when somebody lights a candle, as in a church, it is a symbolic act. A fairy-tale is not only a story for children, it has a symbolic function; it can help children to overcome a fear or to structure their perception of the world. Language often has a symbolic function. For instance, the expression 'How do you do? is not a question to discover how well you are. It has a symbolic social function and prepares for a dialogue or other verbal contact. Language expresses in a symbolic way what we feel.

Bibliography

Aimard, P. 1982. *L'Enfant et son langage*. Villeurbanne: Simep Editions.

Akoun, A. *et al.* 1971. *La psychologie moderne de A à Z*. Paris: CEPL.

Alexander, G. 1976. *Eutonie. Ein Weg der körperlichen Selbsterfahrung*. München: Kösel Verlag.

Ancelin Schützenberger, A. 1970. *Précis de psychodrame*. Paris: Editions universitaires.

Ancelin Schützenberger, A. 1981. *Le jeu de rôle*. Paris: Editions ESF.

Anzieu, D. 1977. *Psychanalyse et langage*. Paris: Dunod.

Anzieu, D. 1982. *Le travail psychanalytique dans les groupes*. 1. *cadre et processers*. Paris: Bordas.

Anzieu, D. 1984. *Le groupe et l'inconscient* I. *L'imaginaire groupal* . Paris: Bordas.

Apollinaire, G. 1915. 'Case d'Armons'. *Oeuvres poétiques*. Paris: Editions Gallimard, 1956.

Aucher, M.L. 1977a. *L'Homme sonore*. Paris: Epi.

Aucher, M.L. 1977b. *Les Plans d'expression*. Paris: Epi.

Aucher, M.L. 1987. *En corps chanté*. Paris: Hommes & Groupes éditeurs.

Balmary, M. 1986. *Le Sacrifice interdit*. Paris: Grasset.

Baron, G. 1981. *Mémoire vivante*. Paris: Le Centurion.

Besse, H. 1974. 'Les exercices de conceptualisation ou la réflexion grammaticale au niveau 2' in *VIC*. 2/1974. Saint-Cloud: CREDIF.

Besse, H. and R. Gallisson. 1980. *Polémique en didactique*. Paris: CLE International.

Blatner, A. 1973. *Acting in. Practical Application of Psychodramatic Methods*. New York: Springer Publishing Company.

Boal, A. 1980a. *Théâtre de l'opprimé*. Paris: François Maspero.

Boal, A. 1980b. *Stop! C'est magique*. Paris: Hachette.

Boal, A. 1983. *Jeux pour acteurs et non-acteurs*. Paris: François Maspero.

Boon, H., Y. Davrou, and J.-C. Macquet. 1976. *La sophrologie*. Paris: Retz.

Bour, P. 1972. *Le psychodrame et la vie*. Neuchâtel: Delachaux et Niestlé.

Calbris, G. and J. Montredon. 1975. *Approche rythmique, intonative et expressive du français langue étrangère*. Paris: CLE International.

Calbris, G. and J. Montredon. 1981. *Oh là là. Expression intonative et minique*. Paris: CLE International.

Callamand, M. 1973. *L'intonation expressive*. Paris: BELC.

Callamand, M. 1981. *Méthodologie de l'enseignement de la prononciation*. Paris: CLE International.

Caré, J.M. and F. Debyser. 1978. *Jeu, langue et créativité*. Paris: Hachette/Larousse.

Claudel, P. 1957. 'Visages radieux'. *Oeuvres poétiques*. Paris: Editions Gallimard.

David, P. 1981. *La séance de psychanalyse*. Paris: Armand Colin.

Davis, P. and M. Rinvolucri. 1990. *The Confidence Book*. Harlow: Longman.

Davrou, Y. and J.-C. Macquet. 1978. *Le guide pratique de la sophrologie*. Paris: Retz.

de Ajuriaguerra, J. 1977. *Manuel de Psychiatrie de l'enfant*. Paris: Masson.

Delattre, P. 1965. *Comparing the phonetic features of English, German, Spanish and French*. Heidelberg: Gross Verlag.

Delattre, P. 1969. 'L'intonation par les oppositions', in *Le français dans le monde (LFDM)* no. 64, pp. 6–13.

Desnos, R. 1944. *Chantefables et Chantefleurs*. Paris: Gründ.

Dolto, F. 1985. 'L'enfant, le langage et le corps', (interview in *Le Journal des psychologues* no. 5).

Dolto, F. 1987. *Tout est langage*. Paris: Vertiges du Nord/Carrere.

Dropsy, J. 1973. *Vivre dans son corps*. Paris: Epi.

Dufeu, B. 1982a. 'Vers une pédagogie de l'être: la pédagogie relationnelle', in *Die Neueren Sprachen*. Vol. 81, pp. 267–89.

Dufeu, B. 1982b. 'La grammaire intentionnelle', in Schultz, F. (ed.).

Dufeu, B. 1983a. 'La psychodramaturgie linguistique ou l'apprentissage de la langue par le vécu', in *LFDM* no. 175, pp. 36–45.

Dufeu, B. 1983b. 'Techniques de jeu de rôle', in *LFDM* no. 176, pp. 69–74.

Dufeu, B. 1983c. 'Haben und Sein im Fremdsprachenunterricht', in Prengel, A.

Dufeu, B. (ed.) 1985. *Teilnehmeraktivierende Lernformen im Fremd-sprachenunterricht für Erwachsene.* Mainz: Universität Mainz.

Dufeu, B. 1986. 'Rythme et expression', in *LFDM* no. 205, pp. 62–70. et 208 (avril 1987), pp. 12–13.

Dufeu, B. 1987a. *Neue Lehr-und Lernformen.* Mainz: Universität Mainz.

Dufeu, B. 1987b. 'Anders lehren, anders lernen oder der Exotismus im Fremdsprachenunterricht', in B. Dufeu (ed.) *Neue Lehr-und Lernformen und ihre Umsetzung im Fremdsprachenunterricht für Erwachsene.* Berichte und Beiträge zur wissenschaftlichen Weiterbildung Vol. 22, pp. 15–43. Mainz: Universität Mainz.

Dufeu, B. 1990. 'Sensibilisation à certaines approches du jeu de rôle', in *AFLS Newsletter* no. 25, pp. 22–28.

Dufeu, B. 1992. *Sur les chemins d'une pédagogie de l'être.* Mainz: Editions Centre de Psychodramaturgie.

Dufeu, B. 1993. 'Un exercice ouvert: La prison', in *LFDM* no. 259, pp. 56–61.

Dufeu, B., M. Dufeu, and D. Feldhendler. 'Psychodrame et apprentissage des langues', in *Le Journal du Psychodrame* no. 7, 1991, pp. 51–55.

Dufeu, M. 1985. 'Teilnehmeraktivierende Lernformen im Fremdsprachenunterricht für Erwachsene. Workshop Französisch II' in Dufeu, B. (ed.).

Dufeu, M. 1989. *Vers une pédagogie du contact ou vers une approche de l'enseignement des langues à la lumière de la Gestalt.* Mainz: Editions Centre de Psychodramaturgie.

Ehrenfried, L. 1980. *De l'éducation du corps à l'équilibre de l'esprit.* Paris: Aubier.

Eliot, A., M. Eliade, J. Campbell, and E. M. Bührer. 1976. *Myths.* Maidenhead: McGraw-Hill.

Feldhendler, D. 1983. 'Expression Dramaturgique', in *LFDM* no. 176, pp. 45–51.

Feldhendler, D. 1988. 'Le théâtre journal vivant', in *LFDM* no. 220, pp. 56–61.

Feldhendler, D. 1989. *Psychodrama und Theater der Unterdrückten.* Frankfurt: Puppen und Masken.

Feldhendler, D. 1990. 'Dramaturgie et interculturel', in *LFDM* no. 234, pp. 50–60.

Feldhendler, D. 1991. 'Das Leben in Szene setzen! Ansätze für eine fremdsprachliche Dramaturgie', in *Die Neueren Sprachen* 2/1991, pp. 137–53.

Ferenczi, V. 1978. *Psychologie, langage et apprentissage.* Paris: Didier.

Franzke, E. 1985. *Märchen und Märchenspiel in der Psychotherapie.* Bern: Verlag Hans Huber.

Freud, S. 1951. *Essais de psychanalyse.* Paris: Payot.

Freud, S. 1968. *Introduction à la psychanalyse.* Paris: Payot.

Fulghum, R. 1989. *Alles, was Du wirklich wissen muss, hast Du schon als Kind gelernt.* München: Goldman.

Fustier, M. 1978. *Pratique de la créativité.* Paris: Editions ESF.

Galand, S. and J. Salomé. 1984. *Les Mémoires de l'oubli.* Plombières-les-Dijon: Le Regard Fertile.

Galisson, R. 1980. *D'hier à aujourd'hui la didactique des langues étrangères.* Paris: CLE International.

Garnier, P. 1981. *Le psychodrame, une psychothérapie analytique.* Paris: Editions ESF.

Geissmann, P. and R. Durand de Bousingen. 1968. *Les méthodes de relaxation.* Bruxelles: Dessart et Mardaga.

Ginger, S. 1987. *La Gestalt une thérapie de contact.* Paris: Hommes et Groupes éditeurs.

Goldman, E. and D. Morrison. 1984. *Psychodrama: Experience and Process.* Dubuque, Iowa: Kendall/Hunt Publishing Company.

Graham, C. 1978. *Jazz Chants.* Oxford: Oxford University Press.

Guberina, P. 1965. 'La méthode audio-visuelle structuro-globale', in *Revue de Phonétique Appliquée.* No. 1, pp. 35–64.

Guberina, P. 1972. *Restricted Bands of Frequencies in Auditory Rehabilitation of the Deaf.* Zagreb: Institute of Phonetics.

Howatt, A.P.R. 1984. *A History of English Language Teaching.* Oxford: Oxford University Press.

Hugo, V. 1825. 'Les Orientales'. *Oeuvres Poétiques.* Paris, Nouvelle Edition Illustrée and Editions Gallimard.

Jacobson, E. 1929. *Progressive Relaxation.* Chicago: University of Chicago Press.

Jacobson, E. 1962. *You Must Relax.* New York: McGraw-Hill.

Jakobson, R. 1963. *Essais de linguistique générale.* Paris: Editions de Minuit.

Jousse, M. 1974. *L'anthropologie du geste.* Paris: Editions Gallimard.

Jousse, M. 1975. *La manducation de la parole.* Paris: Editions Gallimard.

Jung, C.G. 1964. *L'homme et ses symboles.* Paris: Robert Laffont.
Jung, C.G. 1979. *L'homme à la découverte de son âme.* Paris: Payot.

Kaes, R. *et al.* 1979. *Fantasme et formation.* Paris: Bordas.
Kaes, R. *et al.* 1982. *Le travail psychanalytique dans les groupes. 2. Les voies de l'élaboration.* Paris: Bordas.
Klein, W. 1989. *L'acquisition de langue étrangère.* Paris: Armand Colin.
Korzybski, A. 1941. *General semantics, Psychiatry, Psychotherapy and Prevention.* Chicago: Institute of General Semantics.
Krashen, S.D. 1982. *Principle and Practice in Second Language Acquisition.* Oxford: Pergamon Press.
Krashen, S.D. 1983. *The Natural Approach.* Oxford: Pergamon Press.

Lacan, J. 1966. *Ecrits I.* Paris: Seuil.
Lavater, W. 1965. *Le Petit Chaperon Rouge.* Paris: Adrien Maeght Editeur.
Lemoine, G. and P. Lemoine. 1972. *Le psychodrame.* Paris: Laffont.
Lerède, J. 1980. *Suggérer pour apprendre.* Montréal: Presses de l'Université du Québec.
Leutz, G. 1974. *Psychodrama. Theorie und Praxis.* Berlin: Springer Verlag.
Leutz, G. 1985. *Mettre sa vie en scène.* Paris: Epi.
Lozanov, G. *Suggestology and Outlines of Suggestopedy.* New York: Gordon and Breach.

Maley, A. and A. Duff. 1976. *Variations on a Theme.* Cambridge: Cambridge University Press.
Maley, A. and A. Duff. 1978. *Drama Techniques in Language Teaching.* Cambridge: Cambridge University Press.
Mannoni, O. 1969. *Clefs pour l'Imaginaire ou l'Autre Scène.* Paris: Seuil.
Marzin, Y. 1989. in 'Radioscopie' on 30 April 1981.
Meschonnic, H. 1982. *Critique du rythme.* Lagrasse: Verdier.
Middendorf, I. 1984. *Der erfahrbare Atem. Eine Atemlehre.* Paderborn: Jungfermann Verlag.
Miller, A. 1983. *Le Drame de l'enfant doué.* Paris: PUF.
Miller, H. 1971. *The Smile at the Foot of the Ladder.* Paris: Editions Buchet/Chastel, p. 54, New Directions Publishing Corporation 1975.
Moget, M.T. and P. Neveu. 1975. *De vive Voix.* Livre de l'étudiant. Paris: Didier.

Moirand, S. 1982. *Enseigner à communiquer en langue étrangère.* Paris: Hachette.

Moreno, J.L. 1914. *Einladung zu einer Begegnung.* Wien: Auzegruber Verlag.

Moreno, J.L. 1970. *Fondements de la sociométrie.* Paris: PUF.

Moreno, J.L. 1973. *The Theater of Spontaneity.* New York: Beacon House.

Moreno, J.L. 1987. *Psychothérapie de groupe et psychodrame.* Paris: PUF.

Morgan, J. and M. Rinvolucri. 1988. *The Q Book.* Harlow: Longman.

Moskowitz, G. 1978. *Caring and Sharing in the Foreign Language Class: A Sourcebook on Humanistic Techniques.* Rowley, Mass.: Newbury House.

Petzold, H. 1982. *Dramatische Therapie.* Stuttgart: Hippokrates Verlag.

Prengel, A. (ed.). 1983. *Gestaltpädagogik.* Weinheim: Beltz Verlag.

Prevert, J. 1949. *Paroles.* Paris: Editions Gallimard.

Rager, G.R. 1973. *Hypnose, sophrologie et médecine.* Paris: Artheme Fayard.

Richaudeau, F. 1975. *Les secrets de la communication efficace.* Paris: Retz-CEPL.

Richelle, M. 1976. *L'acquisition du langage.* Bruxelles: Dessart et Mardaga.

Rinvolucri, M. 1984. *Grammar Games.* Cambridge: Cambridge University Press.

Rivarol, A. 1784. *Discours sur l'universalité de la langue française.* Paris: Larousse 1936.

Salomé, J. 1986. *Relation d'aide et formation à l'entretien.* Lille: Presses Universitaires de Lille.

Schmidbauer, W. 1977. *Die hilflosen Helfer.* Hamburg: Rowohlt.

Schultz, F. (ed.). 1982. *Erstellen von Lehrmaterial.* Mainz: Universität Mainz.

Schultz, J.H. 1965. *Le training autogène.* Paris: PUF.

Schultz, J.H. 1977. *Übungsheft für das autogene Training.* Stuttgart: Georg Thieme.

Sheleen, L. 1983. *Théâtre pour devenir ... autre.* Paris: Epi.

Silva, J. and B. Goldman. 1990. *The Silva Mind Control Method of Mental Dynamics.* New York: Simon and Schuster.

Smith, S. 1937. *A Good Time was Had by All*. London: Cape/ Penguin.

Souriau, E. 1950. *Les deux cent mille situations dramatiques*. Paris: Flammarion Editeur.

Stevick, E. 1990. *Humanism in Language Teaching*. Oxford: Oxford University Press.

Tardieu, J. 1951. *Monsieur Monsieur*. Paris: Editions Gallimard.

Tomatis, A. 1963. *L'Oreille et le langage*. Paris: Seuil.

Tomatis, A. 1991. *Nous sommes tous nés polyglottes*. Paris: Fixot.

Urbain, W. 1972. *L'Expression spontanée et son application à l'apprentissage des langues*. Paris: CESDEL.

Vaughan-Rees, M. 1991. *Speak Out!* London: IATEFL.

Verlaine, P. 1962. *Oeuvres poétiques complètes*. Paris: Editions Gallimard.

Vygotsky, L.S. 1964. *Denken und Sprechen*. Berlin: Fischer Verlag.

Widdowson, H.G. 1990. *Aspects of Language Teaching*. Oxford: Oxford University Press.

Widdowson, H.G. and C.N. Candlin. 1987–94. *Language Teaching*: A Scheme for Teacher Education series. Oxford: Oxford University Press.

Winnicott, D.W. 1971. *Playing with Reality*. London: Routledge.

Woodward, T. 1990. *Models and Metaphors in Language Teacher Training*. Cambridge: Cambridge University Press.

Woodward, T. 1992. *Ways of Training*. Harlow: Longman.

Index

Entries relate to Chapters 1 to 9 and the glossary. References to the glossary are indicated by 'g' and to the notes by 'n'.

Entries are in letter-by-letter alphabetical order, in which spaces between words are ignored in filing; 'inner language' therefore comes before 'in step....'.